WOMEN, MONEY, AND THE ENERGY OF LIFE

Helping women grow in abundance and impact while owning their worth (and staying true to who they are)

WOMEN OF THE WORLD NETWORK®

Compiled by ELLE BALLARD
#1 International Best Selling Author

WOMEN, MONEY, AND THE ENERGY OF LIFE
Helping women grow in abundance and impact while owning their worth
(and staying true to who they are)

Copyright © 2023 by Elle Ballard

Women of the World Network®
35111F Newark Blvd Suite 580
Newark, CA 94560

All rights reserved. No part of this publication may be reproduced distributed or transmitted in any form or by any means including photocopying recording or other electronic or mechanical means without proper written permission of author or publisher, except in the case of brief quotations embodied in critical reviews and certain other noncommercial uses permitted by copyright law.

ISBN 978-1-7365957-3-2 (paperback)

Visit us on line at **www.YourPurposeDrivenPractice.com**
Printed in the United States of America.

WHAT PEOPLE ARE SAYING

"It was just the motivation I needed to believe in myself first but also to remember that I don't have to go at it alone."
-Tiffani Freckleton, RN and Best-Selling Author

«These stories of real women from around the world, told by themselves in an intimate voice, gave me a sense of possibilities and a strong feeling that an abundant life is possible for everyone, regardless of their background.»
-Radha Alina Ionescu, Conscious Love Coach

"This anthology is a timely collection of feminine wisdom around finance...An inspiring must read for women of all ages!"
-Shelby Kottemann, Founder of Love's Nature LLC

"The stories she collected are inspirational, revolutionary, invigorating, and spiritual...The anthology is a highly recommended read for both men and women."
-Terry Philip Wilson, International Best-Selling Author

"These stories provide perspective on uncovering our blind spots and making the right choices."
-Manisha Gupta

"An international approach to living well and finding one's worth"
-Maureen Ryan Blake, Maureen Ryan Blake Media Production

WOMEN, MONEY, AND INFLUENCE

"I was inspired by the courage and motivation of these women to become masters of their lives. Their journey was not always smooth and easy, but they were able to learn and grow from their experiences."
-Brita Peterson, International Best-Selling Author

"Loved every story in the book and saw me in every chapter."
-Uttara Pandya, Director with Melaleuca

"I highly recommend this book to anyone who wants to learn more about the relationship between money and happiness, and how to build a life that's aligned with your values and goals."
-Fernanda Cortes, Graphic Designer

"It makes me realized the true value of my own experiences, encourage me to start with a simple plan, learn from their ups and downs and hope for a brighter future. I hope that every women (and men) will get to read this book!"
-Margie Viaga Calangian, Litigation Support Specialist
Lieff Cabraser Heimann & Bernstein, LLP

CONTENTS

Foreword: Women of the World Network®: Women, Money, and the Energy of Life....... 7

Money and Energy of Life

Money Is the Vital Energy	By Eleonora Demesinova	11
Creating Wealth and Prosperity with the Power of Ginsiinmei® – the Synergies of Truthgoodnessbeauty	By Marsha Cheung Golangco	19
Achieving Wealth the Feminine Way	By Aizhan Kadyr	31
Elevating Financial Confidence in Women	By Sheilla Vidal	37
Manifesting Abundance	By Elle Ballard	45

Living Life on Your Own Terms

Finding Purpose and Meaning in Life	By Miranti Ojong	55
My American Dream: From Immigrant to Entrepreneur	By Alpana Aras-King	63
Live the Life You Love as an Entrepreneur!	By Faye Calangian	75
What's Self-Worth Got to Do with It?	By Mary Ann Faremouth	83
Feeling Secure with Money	By Rita Roushdy	91

Finding Meaning in It All

Love-Hate Relationship with Money	By Jacqueline Clarke	101
Women and Money: Quick Reminders	By Nataly Kolchev	107
New Shoes	By Bonnie M. Russell	111
From Darkness to Sunlight	By Akili Atkinson	117

WOMEN, MONEY, AND INFLUENCE

Thank You..125
Testimonials..127
Reviews...129

FOREWORD
WOMEN OF THE WORLD NETWORK®:
WOMEN, MONEY, AND THE ENERGY OF LIFE

Thank you for picking this beautiful compilation of powerful stories! I am honored and excited to bring you our third edition of the Women of the World Network® Anthologies Series where we share stories of fourteen women from ten countries including USA, Kazakhstan, Russia, Germany, UK, India, Philippines, Egypt, Hong Kong, and Indonesia. This book is not only about having money, but also about being able to choose for yourself how much you want to earn, how much you want to work, how you can create a life your way, and having confidence that you can achieve whatever you are after.

In this edition, we are excited to share fourteen unique, vulnerable, powerful stories on mindset, growth, overcoming, and achieving. Each chapter starts with a personal story and is followed by a biography and contact information on each author. While putting this book together, I asked ladies to share their personal stories and money stories, how their upbringing influenced their life and financial choices, how they changed it, how they grew through it, and how they created the lives they love living. I want to thank all of our participating authors for sharing their stories from the heart with passion and love. A lot of the chapters include 'how-to' to help you grow, achieve your goals, and create a life that you dream of. I know you will learn from these unique and powerful stories. Enjoy!

MONEY AND ENERGY OF LIFE

MONEY IS THE VITAL ENERGY
BY ELEONORA DEMESINOVA

Money is one of the most genius inventions of humanity, and yet one of the most charged phenomena for the majority of people and especially women. My personal view is that money making is not an easy, but interesting job to do, and business men and women should be respected just like doctors, musicians, artists, etc. Money is the vital energy.

Unfortunately, it is not the attitude today due to many prejudices around it. In this respect, let us look at a few aspects. We all get conditioned from day one of our birth by parents, teachers, religions, society, media, etc. **We receive zillions of verbal, non-verbal, mental, and energetic signals in the field. Reflecting on my growing up and watching my nephews and nieces growing up also, what I have seen is the first seven years of life, a child is the most pure, vulnerable, and dependent creature in the world.** Children are like plasticine, so parents can model whatever they want. The ideal situation would be if parents or caregivers just took care, supported, and defended the child without stuffing her or him with their ideas of what is right or wrong, at least for the first seven years.

Watching young children, I observe how playful, total, wise, intelligent, and smart they are. They are absolutely able to think and come to their own conclusions right for that moment. If they are left free to have their own thinking, to make their own mistakes, though it is not about mistakes, it is all about the learning process, then girls and boys grow up free and retain the children's intelligence and wisdom the rest of their life. Parents just need to provide safety and respect their space. In reality, it is very rare. Of course, parents love their children, but unconsciously, they destroy a child's individuality. The good news is that there are many ways to decondition people.

Role of Religion

Religion is another aspect that brings tension in this respect. I have not only read the Bible, the Koran, Hadis, and other religion books, but I have also practiced each one of them in my life. What I discovered is, as a woman, I have a right to choose which religion to practice. In reality, if the family or society is religious, they give no freedom to a little girl from the very beginning. It gets so deeply infiltrated into her being that she does not even realize this dependence. It becomes her identity. She has to be this and that, to do this and that. In the past, all religions were not only against women making money, but were condemning money, condemning being rich and happy. We had to be suffering and that was considered spiritual. Spiritual books teach us to be against ourselves, against our sexuality, which is simply our vital energy. They infiltrate the deepest conditioning that someone or something is always better than me, that I deserve not or less, and fear of being punished by the Lord for being different from what they expect you to be. So, what I am saying is that a lot of resistance to having and making a lot of money comes unconsciously from the religions of our ancestors (parents, grandparents, etc.).

The Bible says, "Whoever is kind to the poor lends to the Lord, and He will reward them for what they have done." To me, it is an absolute encouragement of poverty. And it is easier to control and manipulate poor and unhappy people. It is all about keeping control over people because if you are rich, you are independent, at least financially. Yes, religious people do make good money also, but only within their conditioning. They are not free. All religions say that a woman has to obey first the father, then the brother, then the husband, and that's how making money is an issue for many women. Even if you think it does not bother me, somewhere in the background, this influence is still there. And these are only a few examples.

My Family and Beliefs

Luckily, I did not have much religious influence as I was born in Kazakhstan during the Soviet times. Back then, religion was prohibited in the Soviet Union; however, my parents were still doing some Muslim rituals probably just for keeping tradition. It was something like having a short prayer before or after meals. My parents were absolutely impractical financially wise, like a majority of people back then in my country. This brings us to another aspect, which influences one's money situation. It is the country and society of one's birth. My parents did not care much about having big savings or making more money. In their youth, making business could bring criminal prosecution. My father still had a comparatively good salary as he was the main district doctor. I do not remember my parents making any negative remarks about money; on the contrary, they encouraged my desire to earn money. My first job was watering trees in the school yard. I was thirteen years old when I asked my school principal if they had any job for me during the summer vacation. And she said that I could water trees and be paid for that. I was very excited! I remember this happy and warm feeling when I received the first salary in my life. It was quite a big amount for a schoolgirl. So the next summer, I worked again, in the kindergarten, helping to take care of children. And again, so much joy and satisfaction I received from the job done and being rewarded. So it is very important that parents do not interfere in their children's good intentions and they do not condition them with their own beliefs and worries. However, it is not completely possible, and we still get programmed this or the other way by our surrounding, parents, friends, state, etc. The good news is we can decondition ourselves through meditation techniques to clear up these imprints.

Role and Impact of Women

I have travelled and lived abroad extensively, and one thing I've noticed while watching women's lives in different countries is the level of financial stability, prosperity, and overall wealth of a country is directly connected with the attitude to women in that country. If we have a look at the world map and see countries where women take an active part in the lives of their societies in government, business, medicine, education, etc., we recognize that that country is the most successful. Once a woman takes full responsibility over her life, it changes everything and everyone around her. If women become free, then men become free too, and the whole world becomes free. My country is a former colony of the Russian empire. This fact gives an additional burden and conditioning on people because they were considered to be kind of second-class people, which is a nationwide trauma. If someone's sense of dignity is broken, it is hard to totally concentrate on rising well-being. We just recently received independence, only thirty years ago, and you can see the high difference between people born then and now. Young women are freer and more active than their mothers. Just thirty years of freedom makes a huge difference. The good news is anyone, no matter what age and social position, can clear up from the old programs if there is a strong desire to do so. The earlier we start, the better.

However, women still run across a lot of obstacles. They are being paid less than men in general, get mistreated, violated, etc. And when I ask myself why these things are still happening today, I see that many women simply do not take responsibility. They are stuck in past patterns. They allow this dependency, not to confuse it with support, on husbands, their men, and bosses because it is the way to escape from reality but being detached traumatizes them even more.

I work as a trauma therapist, consulting with people from all over the world, mainly women. They come with different issues, but one thing that unites them all is a strong desire for realization. They took responsibility and asked for support. This differs them. My job is to help them to get rid of harmful beliefs and conditionings. And it is not difficult at all if only one makes a real decision and is dedicated to breaking free. I learn a lot from each client too. In the session, we find the root of the problem. Mainly it is a trauma; we heal it and add a new habit or another way of looking at things. We learn the new way to live life, not taking things too seriously. Then making money becomes a part of a creative and happy life.

Impact of Unhealed Trauma

Unhealed trauma leads to another one and so on and so forth. And then life becomes like walking in a circle. As part of a grown-up individual's responsibility, financial wealth is a must. If one does not have enough money or assets, it means she or he is not quite grown up and is expecting others to take responsibility for her or him. It is like a child who is needy and completely dependent on his parents. So, the first step to make is to take responsibility. In fact, it includes covering unsatisfied needs left from the past and especially from childhood.

I have one example from my childhood. Once my mother and I were shopping and I saw a beautiful dress. I asked her to buy it for me, but her answers were firm and angry. "Not this time, I do not have enough money." And it happened several times. Of course, over time, the feeling of needing something and not being able to satisfy the need arose. Also, it locked for years from asking anything for myself, and I would sit and wait until she, or other adults, initiated things for me. My mother did not guess what I felt as I did not express my feelings. For sure, she would have done something to get that dress for me.

When I grew up, I bought a beautiful dress I wanted. And the trick is, at the moment of the purchase, I stopped for a moment and started to feel my feelings, bringing whole awareness into that precise moment. I felt that that need from my distant childhood was being transformed, and I received an important knack that I can fulfill my needs without having any expectations from others. And the second important knowing was that I can ask myself for support. In psychology, the small inner me is called an inner child. It is absolutely necessary to get connected with my inner me. So, any lack, including the lack of money, reflects an inner need, which may be satisfied by looking inside, watching, and bringing total awareness into it. No one can give to you what you cannot give yourself. Each one of us is a unique individual; that is why there is no universal method. Can you add how you worked on deprogramming your money attitudes?

Money Awareness Technique

In the end, I will present one of the techniques that has helped to get rid of tension around money by bringing deeper awareness into the subject. It can be practiced any time until all the charge is gone.

Ready? Here We Go:

- Make sure that nobody interrupts you for sixty minutes.
- Switch off the phone.
- Now, take all YOUR cash around the house, put it on the table, and staying present and conscious, then take it in your hands and feel what arises inside.
- Is there any resistance receiving, fear of loss, pain or maybe you are feeling greedy? Maybe there is joy and satisfaction.
- What is there in your body? Maybe some itching starts in some part of the body or a headache appears. Feel it. Feel your body, watch your thoughts, feel your emotions. Do not escape, stay present.
- Write down on paper your emotions, body feelings, all the thoughts in this very moment.
- Then slowly put the money back, like giving it away. And again, feel what is happening. Is there any resistance to giving away, any fears, or on the contrary, liberation. Feel staying present.
- Write down whatever is there in the body, thoughts, emotions.
- And do it several times, receiving and giving back, and then writing down whatever arises. Do it until you feel unburdened and light. In the end,

you will feel happy. Your energy will become playful; you will become joyful.

In conclusion, it is my wish that women would know that they already have what they need to reach high awareness and consciousness levels and who can easily achieve financial well-being. May you build a joyful connection and fulfilling connection with your money.

Eleonora Demesinova

Eleonora Demesinova works as a trauma and crisis therapist and Osho meditation facilitator. Prior to joining therapy and mindfulness path, she worked as a projects business manager in the Water Treatment Facility (WTF) project of Tengizchevroil joint venture (TCO), which is a part of Global Chevron Corporation, a worldwide oil and gas company. Eleonora led the business department for five years. The department provided purchasing, contracting, cost control, supply chain, and human resources services to the WTF project. She finished a lot of business skills, projects, financial and supervisor development courses, got diploma certified in a number of projects professions, having been trained in the USA, UK, Kazakhstan, and Russia. After working fifteen years in TCO in sdifferent positions like management team executive coordinator, contracting specialist, projects business analyst, deputy business manager in TCO Crude oil export project, and TCO WTF business manager, she decided to leave the company for inner research work. She works as a therapeutic session giver since 2012, having finished many therapy, meditation facilitation, energy work courses like body mind balance, no mind, reference point therapy, and many more. She also organizes mediation groups, inviting world-known Osho therapists. Eleonora successfully applies knowledge from these seemingly different spheres (oil and gas business and spiritual growth) to help her clients to enhance and deepen their life experiences. She lived in India for seven years learning and practicing meditation. She also travelled a lot around the world.

Email Address: **amolahappy9@gmail.com**
Phone Number + 7 776 765 2997, WhatsApp, telegram, viber + 7 968 966 8262
Facebook page(s): Amola amola, Eleonora Demesinova, Make Your Life Beautiful.
Instagram: **eleonoraamola**
YouTube Channel: Amola, Амола

Love, Harmony & Prosperity to you & your family
Marsha 2023

CREATING WEALTH AND PROSPERITY WITH THE POWER OF GINSIINMEI® – THE SYNERGIES OF TRUTHGOODNESSBEAUTY
BY MARSHA CHEUNG GOLANGCO

Growing Up with Affluence, Prestige and Influence Won't Guarantee a Lifetime of Wealth and Prosperity

In life, there is no guarantee that, if you are fortunate to be born into a wealthy family, you will be rich for the rest of your life. In fact, it will be a hinderance to your own success if there is too much financial dependence on others.

My own story is a classic example of entitlement and dependence. I was born in Hong Kong as a member of the Cheung family, a prominent family during the British colonial era. I am the youngest child of my mother's seven children and number ten of my father's thirteen children. My father had two wives, a common practice at that time; we all lived harmoniously together in a five-story mansion at the mid-level of Victoria Peak.

The Cheung family was a traditional, extended Chinese family; I lived with my grandparents, my father with his two wives and thirteen children, my three uncles and aunts and their children, a total of forty family members. Together with thirty plus domestic helpers, I lived with more than seventy people in the same house. It was a life of security, comfort, abundance, and prestige.

Family Financial Support and Dependence

Money was never an issue; there was great wealth to provide for food, lodging, clothing, schooling, and a monthly allowance. The Cheung family was a well-known 'old family' in Hong Kong, with business first in the pharmaceutical industry, and then in real estate development. It was my father and his brothers who migrated to Hong Kong during the Second World War and started a business. They made use of the free-for-all opportunity after the war and created great wealth during that time.

In return of their good fortune, the Cheung family became very philanthropic. Huge sums of money were donated to charities, especially to many educational institutions from elementary to high schools to colleges, including the Cheung Cheuk Shen High School, named after my grandfather, and the auditorium in the Chinese University of Hong Kong, also named after my grandfather.

Growing up with wealth and family prominence gave me a sense of security and pride. As a child, I was given the best of everything; I never had to worry about being hungry, or lacking material goods, and never had any prejudice nor discrimination against me and other family members. As one of the richest and most influential families in Hong Kong, the Cheung family members were always admired and respected.

The Transformational Path from Financial Dependence to Independence

It is an irony in my life that growing up wealthy didn't give me the advantages that were designed by elders of my family. Despite my high educational achievements with numerous college degrees, I was not motivated to make an extraordinary career. I was satisfied with low-paying jobs without any desire for high positions with high pay. I always counted on receiving a family inheritance on maintaining a lifestyle of what I considered freedom, leisure, and fun.

My turning point came when a close friend invited me to attend a self-discovery program. I gradually realized that I had been wasting precious time and energy focusing on small-life achievements and my dependence on others for financial support. I was surprised to find out that I was a person of multiple talents with something unique and valuable to offer.

Shifting my paradigm in finances gave me an unexpected accomplishment in becoming a known Feng Shui expert in the building industry. Due to my early family introduction to the ancient discipline of Feng Shui, I was able to integrate that knowledge into the modern designing and building processes in the construction of structures, helping builders to greatly enhance their products. With the additional training as a green building professional, I was able to create a unique, successful consulting business that provides valuable services to build quality and healthy living environments. My additional claim to fame was in publishing three books, *The Power of Feng Shui Trilogy*, and I recently became an international bestselling author in five anthologies.

Creating and Attracting Wealth–Health Is Wealth

There is a saying from the ancient wisdom of Feng Shui that says, "Health is Wealth."

This is a profound teaching that sums up that, to create wealth and to attract wealth, one must be physically, mentally, emotionally, financially, and spiritually healthy to attract wealth to come your way! In addition, the environment of doing business and the type of business must be healthy, positive, and beneficial to society.

There are many approaches to being successful in life. Feng Shui leads the way of creating and attracting a successful life. As a complete and holistic living system, feng shui provides a spiritual and yet profoundly practical application in modern-day healthy living.

Literally translated as wind and water, Feng Shui is a complex network of concepts based on the idea that a universal life force or energy, called Chi, affects people positively or negatively, depending on their physical state and surroundings. It is the energy that exists in all living matter and binds us together. The field of Feng Shui honors Chi, the essence of which is creating people and their environment.

A healthy and well environment creates and attracts healthy people and business; therefore, creating wealth and attracting the wealthy chi.

It is important to know that many aspects of Feng Shui are metaphysical and give a spiritual point of view. However, they are practical, indicate common sense, and can be used as a resource in creating the highest-quality holistic condition that is referred to as *GinSiinMei*, TruthGoodnessBeauty.

The Power of GinSiinMei, TruthGoodnessBeauty

GinSiinMei signifies the highest quality of life. Translated directly to Truth, Goodness, Beauty, it is a field of life synergies consisting of all these three highest qualities blended together and existing in our own lives. It is critical that we are aware of its existence so we can ignite this valuable power from within us.

What is GinSiinMei?

GinSiinMei is the highest level of quality of life and has been known in ancient Chinese culture for thousands of years. It is a collective energy field of three important qualities, Gin (truth); Siin (Goodness); Mei (Beauty).

- **Gin by itself is Truth** – the quality of being true – in a state of truthfulness; authentic; not fake
- **Siin by itself is Goodness** –the quality of being good–do good; do no harm–act in kindness, love and compassion
- **Mei by itself is Beauty**–the quality of being beautiful–inner and outer beauty–being healthy in every aspect of self; community; environment and planet Earth

These three qualities are connected. They are joined and do not separate themselves from each other. It is the synergy of all three acting and working together to bring out the best possible outcomes. They are all connected in a magical place/domain that creates unexpected results that have a profound impact in our existing world and beyond.

Empowering the world with GinSiinMei starts with ourselves; we are the source of this power. When we are being GinSiinMei, we are in the domain of loving kindness with compassion. We will act with GinSiinMei and do GinSiinMei deeds resulting in a world of GinSiinMei. *Having a world GinSiinMei is fulfilling our ultimate vision of living a way of life that is beneficial to all living matters in our world.*

We all have GinSiinMei within us; it is a matter of connecting with this inner power. It starts with us being healthy, physically, mentally, and spiritually. When we have a loving heart and a clear mind, we become aware of the inner power within us.

We Are the Source of Our GinSiinMei

As mystical as it is, we do not know how GinSiinMei works. A conscious awareness would be a start, then a conscious choice of a desire for GinSiinMei will evolve. It is just like lighting the first candle in a dark room, causing the rippling effect to eventually light up the whole room. We are the source of this power, generating from within, and sharing from self to ignite others to get in touch with theirs. Eventually, transforming the world.

Just imagine what the world would be like if we all lived a life constantly in touch of the power of GinSiinMei, serving humanity and being a contribution to the world that we all love and live in!

A Simple Approach to Get in Touch with Your GinSiinMei

Do No Harm–Do Good

The Harm-Good model is a profound and proactive way to be in touch with our inner power of GinSiinMei. This could be applied in every aspect of our healthy living to create and attract Wealth or Wealthy Chi. This model gives us a reference for the impact of our daily behavior that we may not be mindful or aware of. It is important to know that for every action we take, there are positive and negative consequences that will impact ourselves and others. Living a healthy, vibrant life involves self-generative monitoring efforts. We learn to be acutely aware of each action we take and its impact on ourselves and others.

Here are some self-reflective questions to help build healthy, daily practices:

What are the harmful effects of our actions to us and others?
What are the beneficial effects of our actions to us and others?
What daily actions will reduce doing harm?

What daily actions will increase doing good?

Based on this exploration, what actions do I choose to take?

Please note: GinSiinMei is a created word generated by the author. This word represents three words, Truth, Goodness, Beauty in Chinese characters.

GinSiinMei is trademarked by the author Marsha Cheung Golangco.

Circular Economy and Social Entrepreneurship

Like the ancient wisdom of GinSiinMei, both circular economy and social entrepreneurship are two modern business approaches and practices that are beneficial to society while creating wealth and prosperity.

Similar to GinSiinMei, both circular economy and social entrepreneurship focus on Doing No Harm and Doing Good in different levels of one's life: Self, Family, Work or Business, Communities, Nation and the World.

Circular economy is an emerging business system that is getting popular with an emphasis on sustainability, which is "development that meets the needs of the present without compromising the well-being of future generations" as defined by the World Commission on Environment and Development in 1987. The Sustainable Development Goals are explained in a collection of seventeen goals put forth by the United Nations as a universal call-to-action to end poverty, protect the planet, and ensure that all people enjoy peace and prosperity by 2030.

Just like the Do No Harm/Do Good approach of GinSiinMei, sustainability is to reduce the harm by reducing the traditional business practices of wastefulness, pollution, over-depletion of natural resources, and overconsumption. Sustainable development designs also increase the Doing Good by providing a supportive system of well-being for the three Ps–People, Planet, Profit.

Circular economy is a desirable, local-to-global economic environment based on sustainable development designs in preventing the negative impacts of business and promoting the positive impacts to the thee Ps–People, Planet, Profit!

Social Entrepreneur is an individual business owner who desires to create wealth with the intention of giving the profit back to society. In other words, to make money to promote the well-being of others, as in the three Ps–People, Planet, Profit.

It is important to note that the kind of businesses we conduct are positive and beneficial, such as helping people to do well, rather than being harmful and hurtful to others in society and the world.

The Integration of GinSiinMei, Circular Economy, and Social Entrepreneurship Create the Synergy that Attracts Wealth and Prosperity

Getting in Touch with My Inner Power of GinSiinMei- TruthGoodnessBeauty

As a transformed person living an extraordinary, fulfilled life, it did not occur to me that I am also a human being traveling the inevitable phase of my life path. I remember facing the crossroad not too long ago where I needed to decide if I would give up my successful business and go into retirement or to continue to be proactive and productive as usual. I could imagine myself traveling to places of interest, relaxing on a cruise ship, or just going through every day without the stress of working. I was ready to wind down and let go of being productive. Then I got in touch with my inner power of GinSiinMei–the synergies of TruthGoodnessBeauty.

It was a moment of truth for me! I am not ready or willing to go into hibernation yet! I still must fulfill my ultimate purpose of life: **to be of service to humanity and be a contribution to the world!**

Living My Ultimate Purpose of Life in Creating Wealth and Prosperity

To live my ultimate life purpose, I actively sustain a healthy, daily lifestyle of self-care: physically, mentally, emotionally, spiritually, and financially. It is important for us to sustain the wellness of self and encourage others to take good care of themselves to be healthy. This is a good time to connect the dots of my lifetime achievement and form a partnership/alliance with others who walk a similar path. Together we could make a bigger difference for ourselves and our world!

Having a World of GinSiinMei Is Beneficial to All!

Today, instead of retiring, I am actively pursuing personal, business, and community developments to be a proactive social entrepreneur. This is fulfilling my ultimate purpose of doing business--that is, to create wealth to be circulated to support others and the well-being of our society and to our world. This financial development would be intimately connected to the ancient wisdom of GinSiinMei- TruthGoodnessBeauty.

GinSiinMei will cultivate the environment of beneficial *Chi*, putting us in a positive life path for ourselves and others. Together with the modern concepts of circular economy and social entrepreneurship, a powerful alliance in creating and attracting wealth beneficial for all.

Marsha Cheung Golangco

Marsha Cheung Golangco is a bestselling author, speaker, and consultant in Environmental Feng Shui and Sustainable Green Building Advisory. She is also a social entrepreneur and a long-time community advocate. Her mission is to promote a harmonious world that works for all. For many years, Marsha has used her knowledge and wisdom in helping others to create favorable and healthy living environments for a better quality of life.

Committed to a life-time contribution to the ongoing global peace and the sustainable green movement, Marsha continues to develop a local-to-global collaboration through her business and community advocacy. She serves in many local-to-global organizations, including USGBC (United States Green Building Council, East Bay, California), president of the board of director of APAPA (Asian American Islander American Public Affairs Association) Bay Area region, and cofounders of Sustainable Contra Costa and Sustainable Walnut Creek, California.

For her many community contributions, Marsha has received numerous awards, including the President's Award of the Year from the Building Industry Association for her dedication to the advancement of professional women in the building industry. She is a recipient of an Honorable Mention Martin Luther King Jr. Humanitarian Award of the Year 2005 in Contra Costa County, CA, and the Asian American Islander American of the Year (APIA) 2020 recognized by California Legislature Assembly Member Rebecca Bauer-Kahan.

Sharing her knowledge and wisdom in the Eastern culture, Marsha co-authored five bestselling anthologies and is the author of *The Power of Feng Shui Trilogy:*

- *The Power of Feng Shui for Builders*
- *The Power of Feng Shui for Your Life*
- *The Power of Feng Shui for Green Living*

Marsha can be reached at **fengshu888@aol.com or mgolangco@gmail.com**
Website: **www.windwater888.com**
Facebook: **facebook.com/marsha.golangco**
LinkedIn: **www.linkedin.com/in/marsha-golangco**

ACHIEVING WEALTH THE FEMININE WAY
BY AIZHAN KADYR

Have you heard about the connection between material things and spirituality? Spiritual impulses and desires happen first, and then they are followed by their realization in the material world. Spiritual impulses are causes, in this case, affecting changes in the material world.

How to connect matter with spirit?

I often say in my classes that it is important to find the sources of joy and happiness within your soul.

According to one of the most quoted rules of happiness, the rule is 50-40-10. This rule originates from the book *The How of Happiness* by Sonja Lyubomirsky. She says, "Fifty percent of our happiness is determined by genetics, 10 percent by our circumstances, and 40 percent by our internal state of mind."

It is wonderful when a person develops her or his inner state, when she or he is spiritually developed and can subtly feel everything that happens to her or him. Unfortunately, sometimes being on this path, a person can completely break away from reality and go into a "nirvana" state for a long time, forgetting about loved ones and family. The other extreme, which is also inharmonious, is when people think only about material values, engage in hoarding, completely forgetting about their soul and the higher purpose of their destiny. Happiness and harmony need to be in the balance state that is between spirit and matter. Let's talk more about how to get there.

When you know how to listen to your heart, you can easily find a balance between matter and spirit. Let's look at this topic from the point of view of the location of the chakras. The three lower chakras—*manipura, svadhisthana,* and *muladhara*—are located below the heart. They are associated with instincts, passions, material values, as well as our influence in society.

The three upper chakras are higher spiritual values: the throat chakra, *vishuddha,* is responsible for creative self-realization, the third eye or *adzhna* is intuition and higher wisdom, and *sahasrara* is the connection with divine cosmic forces. Why do you think the *anahata* heart chakra is located in the middle between the upper and the lower world, between spirit and matter? It is the heart that is responsible for the balance of these two worlds; it is able to harmonize them.

When we pass life events and experiences through the prism of our heart, then alchemy occurs, something new is born. It is the heart that helps us find the balance between these two aspirations.

This is what I observed in my own life, watching the development of my male counterparts: in the first half of life, they are aimed at sex, making money, and power. Then saturation occurs; after forty to fifty years, men become the most advanced, rich, and successful people, and they begin to engage in charity and patronage.

If they do not do this, they can burn in the fire of their passions, and as a result, lose a lot. Here is what the famous British hippie billionaire, the owner of Virgin Corporation, Richard Branson, who gives a huge part of his income to charity projects, says about charity:

"I believe that it is business that can make this world a better place, as entrepreneurs have skills that government agencies and social services do not have. Every business has to adopt the problem and help solve it. In the short term, this is an additional cost, but trust me, your employees will be much more motivated if they know that the money they help the company make brings happiness to people who need help."

Today, Richard Branson dreams of raising the standard of living in Africa, giving the Internet and telephone to millions of people who are deprived of it, and he also wants to stop global warming.

Branson has been happily married to his second wife, Joan Templeman, for thirty-five years. They became the parents of two children who today already have families of their own.

As my experience of conducting women's trainings and consultations shows, it is women who can influence the spiritual development of their men. It is necessary not to break your partner mentally, not to advise or criticize his actions, but to gently guide his thoughts and reasoning with the right questions and a sincere desire to know the truth of his soul.

When he tells you about his deepest desires, he himself suddenly understands and realizes what he wants so much or has wanted for a long time, but still could not come to realize it fully. Inspired by the support of a woman, he begins to create and directs his energies to the search for a mission and socially significant projects.

In general, it is important for each person to harmoniously develop all three of her or his energy centers in order to live a full life, to be happy, loved, and successful. It is also important for modern women to find their mission and realize their talents, to know and feel that they benefit people. Trainings, practices, and communication with spiritually developed like-minded people help in self-development.

But the process of self-knowledge and self-development is not always smooth and even. Sometimes we soar, as if on wings, inspired by the wind of change, and sometimes life sends us tests that can be perceived as a painful incentive for change. Stress, worries, losses also motivate us; this is a development from despair.

I think it is important for us women to maintain this balance of matter and spirit. You might ask why. There are a lot of positives and benefits when this balance is present, but the most important thing that I want to highlight is, if we do not maintain this balance, we can experience energy burnout and apathy followed by depression. We burn out only when the balance of "give and take" is disturbed, when we flow into one side or the other. It is important for every woman to learn to hear her heart, learn its language, trust it, and follow it!

From Comfort Zone to Miracle Zone through Fears

I wanted to warn you: when you start any process, slipping begins right in the middle. You leave your comfort zone, on which has already been written a lot, and there are always zones of panic fears at the edges of our comfort zones. But once you cross that fine line between the comfort zone and the panic zone, and still move forward, you will enter the miracle zone. This is a magical space where dreams come true.

So, you live in a comfort zone, and as soon as you start moving towards changes, exactly in the middle of the process, you start to stagger and storm. Fear and force majeure events begin to turn you away from your goal, to do everything so that you cannot achieve it. And here you need the energy of overcoming, with the help of which you enter the magical zone, where dreams come true, where what you have long wanted and waited for happens to you. Be willing to step out of your current comfort zone into your magical zone.

Naturally, after you have lived in this magical zone for a while, it gradually becomes your comfort zone. You are already getting used to those lovely miracles that happen to you every day. You can catch yourself thinking:

'once I dreamed of such a life, of such a job, to look like this, to live in this city, to drive such a car.' And it will dawn on you that your life today is what you wanted for yourself and what you thought about in the recent past.

I can't wait to see your magical zone become your comfort zone. You can live the life you dream of and desire and I'd be happy to help you build that bridge between your mind, soul, and body and share all my knowledge and experience with you.

Sources:

Wikipedia (web: **https://en.wikipedia.org/wiki/Richard_Branson#Personal_life**)

Aizhan Kadyr

Aizhan Kadyr was born in Kazakhstan. She has an MBA, ICU master-coach, psychologist, tantra master, author of the book, *From Samurai to Geisha: 33 Lessons of Femininity*, creator of psychological game, "Healing of Love", volunteer of the UN program against violence. She specializes on femininity, burn out, and stress management.

Facebook: **https://www.facebook.com/Aizhulya**
Web: **https://bio.site/aishakadyr**

Gina,
Here's to a life of dignity,
ease and grace!
Sheila Vidal

ELEVATING FINANCIAL CONFIDENCE IN WOMEN
BY SHEILLA VIDAL

How my relationship with money evolved

I'm excited about this book because women and money are two topics that I'm deeply passionate about.

My fascination with money started over twenty years ago. I realized as an adult with a job that I needed to be responsible for my money. My parents and I had just moved to the US. As a new graduate, I was excited to start a career in physical therapy and to build a life for myself that I could be proud of. Being an immigrant who wants to have a good life in America, I have always been interested in how to manage money and the different ways to build assets.

I had some goals then-make enough money to buy a car. Then a house. I also dreamed of supporting my parents in their old age. We are from the Philippines where it's very common for family members who are doing better financially to support other family members who are struggling or those in the US to send money to family back home. I wanted to do well so my parents would not have to work.

After four years working as a physical therapist (PT), I had enough saved to buy a house. And boy was I excited! I couldn't believe my dream of buying a house was coming true. I purchased a three-bedroom, two-bath, single story at the height of the housing boom. I was introduced to my first life insurance, so in case something happened to me, the house would be paid

WOMEN, MONEY, AND INFLUENCE

off. A couple of years later, I married my wonderful husband. I learned more ways to build assets. I learned about mutual funds and trusts and life insurances. I also worked on paying down our debt.

Working in PT, I have seen patients even in their thirties suffer an unexpected, long-term illness or disability, which significantly lowered their quality of life and financial disposition. I just had my daughter and I wanted to make sure this wouldn't happen to us. I knew that it would be wise to be prepared if something happened to me or my husband, so I made it my goal to save as much as I could, which meant taking additional work outside of my main job as a home health PT.

Then the market crashed and my house went underwater. My investments lost money. I was always worried about finances. I felt I needed to work constantly in order to feel secure about our finances. So I would volunteer to work on weekends and take on more patients as a PT.

This became a vicious cycle of stress. Stress from the fear of not making enough and stress from working a lot. As well as the stress of struggling to get pregnant. Overcoming secondary infertility is a story for another day. Suffice it to say that it took a long time for me to get pregnant again, but the baby didn't make it past six weeks. I was depressed, insecure, angry that it happened to me while many women didn't have any trouble at all. I threw myself into working...and trying to get pregnant again.

I finally got pregnant. But our joy didn't last. Our baby died after twenty-four weeks.

This time, I dealt with the loss of our twenty-four-week-old fetus differently. I was kinder to myself, giving myself space to heal from the two fetal losses. It was very difficult emotionally, but necessary. It made me slow down, reflect, read, pray.

I had an epiphany. Life is too short to live without purpose. But what is my purpose? Why am I here? What is my life mission? Going to work to pay the bills is not why we're here. God created every one of us for something bigger than ourselves. To me, there cannot be anything worse than to die without having lived the life we were meant to live. Therefore, I longed to find my purpose, to do something meaningful and impactful with my life. Something I am truly passionate about.

It was during this time that I learned to change my belief about myself, about money, and life in general. What we create and project out into the world starts from within, and the world gives it back to us. What we sow we will reap. When I truly understood what it meant to be a child of God, to be loved and protected by God because that's what God our Father does to all his children, I realized I was capable of more. I could overcome my self-limiting beliefs, my insecurities, and transform my image of what I am into what I could become. **Instead of relying on myself, on my own strength and abilities, which is super scary by the way, I have come to rely on Him and His loving providence. And it's paid off a hundredfold.**

I let Him lead the way, and He made my dreams come true, bigger and better than I ever thought possible. He made life better that I had imagined. I was blessed with a son, my husband was able to retire from his corporate job, and I was able to work from home three days a week, spend more time with my children, even homeschool them. It's important for me and my husband to be present with our children during their early formative years, and we achieved the time freedom to do that.

I was pregnant with my son when I made the decision to trust in God and join the financial service industry as an independent broker. I learned how to improve my finances and create a financial plan so we can live with dignity, ease, and grace. Based on my own studies, experiences, and learning from mistakes, I developed a system of building assets-my financial foundation pyramid that lays down a solid foundation at the bottom, gradually adding on to it as risk tolerance increases. **Having this financial knowledge**

empowered me and gave me confidence in the future. And helping other women achieve the same results became my purpose.

My work as a physical therapist has taught me the nuances of health care and health insurance coverage. The scary reality is that illness does not discriminate among social status, wealth, age, gender, timing, etc., and when it happens, it can be very costly financially, if not devastating.

I've seen the devastating impact of a long-term illness or disability to a person's dignity and pride. When a person loses his independence and ability to take care of himself, it can truly hurt his dignity and pride. Every person deals with this his own way, and some do not want to inconvenience their loved ones. One sure way to maintain as much of our dignity and pride is to plan ahead.

I became obsessed with ensuring that we can maintain our dignity, particularly in situations where we don't have much control, when unexpected things happen. I became a passionate crusader of life insurance with living benefits.

I learned about real clients getting checks in hundreds of thousands of dollars from their policy upon a diagnosis. And I learned about their program for helping people build a business as independent agents. I found that it not only gave me the solutions I was looking for, but it also allowed me to help other women who need them.

Why Women?

When I was newly married, I saw a newspaper ad for a book about financial intimacy. It was authored by a widow and she wrote about how her husband had always reassured her, "Don't worry about a thing, dear" as he had their financial situation under control. Thankfully, she listened to her gut and insisted that they do some planning. It was what saved her after her husband suddenly passed away; get this, only a few months after they had completed the paperwork. Her husband could have left her with an insurmountable amount of debt he had taken for his business with her as cosigner! While he had the best intentions, and she knew that, it still could have been disastrous. That opened my eyes to the need for women to know how to protect themselves by simply knowing what is happening with our money, whether we manage it ourselves or our partner does.

But women are pulled into many directions by our duties and responsibilities that come with raising children, running a household, and working full time.

We tend to put financial planning on the back burner or let our spouse handle it. The result is a **gender gap on financial confidence.** * This means women are less confident and knowledgeable in handling financial, investment, and insurance decisions compared to men.

Combined with lower lifetime earnings (i.e. due to the wage gap, and time away from work to care for children or parents), and the longer lifespan of women, women have a huge problem on their hands: how to make fewer assets last longer.

> *"Women, on average, are expected to live five years longer than men, but accumulate over $100,000 less wealth." Stanford Center on Longevity*

This then became my mission: helping divorced women, widows, the sandwich generation (moms and daughters of parents with caregiving needs like me; I help take care of my dad) to be financially *confident and equipped* with knowledge, as well as a plan for addressing the above problem: making money last longer. **I want women to be able to manage their finances, even after their spouses are gone or unable to do it, so they can continue to take care of those who matter most.**

Here are a few more statistics:

- 45% of women plan to work after they retire or don't plan to retire due to financial reasons. [1]
- Women have 39% higher health costs in retirement than men, and have twice the risk of developing Alzheimer's than men. [2]
- More than 70% of nursing home residents are females. [3]
- 73% women are more likely to leave work to care for family than men. [4]
- After a divorce, a woman's income falls 41% [5]
- Women survive their husbands by fifteen years and 46 % are unable to maintain their standard of living after the death of their spouse compared to men.[6]

My Dignity Plan ensures the 3 Ls are taken care of: Longevity, Long term care and Legacy. These address the four risks we face: dying too soon, getting sick, living a long life, and running out of money.

Who would have thought that fifteen years after I came across that book about financial intimacy for women, I would be helping the same vulnerable demographics? It certainly wasn't planned, as I had forgotten about the book until recently.

I have done exactly what I had intended: I have become financially literate, and I built assets. I protected the people who matter most, and I have financial security. I'm fulfilling my purpose, helping women and living the life I was meant to live. God has truly exceeded all my hopes and expectations.

---

[1] Transamerica Center for Retirement Studies, November 2019.
[2] Pew Research Center, Jan 2020, and Merrill and Age Wave. "Women and Financial Wellness: Beyond the Bottom Line," September 2019.
[3] American Association for LTC Insurance, "Long Term Care-Important Info for Women," 2019.
[4] AARP, "Women More Likely to Take off Work for Caregiving," May 2019.
[5] Ellevest. "What women Can Do about Inequality," November 2018.
[6] The Administration for Community Living. 2018 Profile of older Americans; April 2018; Prudential Insights; "Planning for Retirement: Women in Two-Income Households and Retirement Risk," June 11, 2019.

With intention and *with the right help*, you too can build the life of purpose that you were meant to live, one with dignity, ease, and grace with the people who matter most.

If you need a hand, reach out to me. I will hold your hand and guide you every step of the way. The journey can be rough, and you need someone who has already done it, who knows the terrain, and who will not give up. I am that person.

I want to end by saying, accumulating money is not the ultimate goal, it is simply the means to bless others who cross our path. Let's not miss the point of our life. In my pursuit of success, I came really close. Don't lose sight of real wealth, the real treasure, which we already have all along. To me, it's God first and family second. God makes all things possible; without Him, we will not be. God blesses us with so many great things, so we can bless others and give the glory back to Him.

*If you'd like to read more about the gender gap in financial confidence, here are some resources:

The Gender Gap on Financial Confidence by Sheilla Vidal.

What's Behind the Financial Literacy Gender Gap? These Academics Say They've Found an Answer by MarketWatch.

Financial Literacy and Wellness among US Women: The Gender Gap from TIAA Institute.

Closing a Gender Gap: Financial Literacy Is not Enough from Stanford Center on Longevity.

Sheilla Vidal

Sheilla is a Bay Area resident, born and raised in the Philippines, who came to the US over twenty years ago with big dreams and an even bigger heart. She is a physical therapist/ financial strategist at Live With Dignity Insurance Services. She is an avid learner and creative problem solver. She loves to support and see other women succeed.

Her family is everything to her, and she loves spending time with her family, hiking to waterfalls, reading, writing, cooking, being inspired, watching the sunset, and connecting with like-minded individuals. She currently homeschools her youngest and enjoys being a teacher of life to her kids. You can reach her for questions, comments, or to get her financial education materials through:

Free eBooks: 5 Financial Considerations for Busy Women and Caregivers, Recession Proofing Your Retirement, How to Fund A Worry Free Retirement, Retirement Income Calculator, and Financial Checklist for Widows and Widowers **https://linktr.ee/sheillavidal**

https://www.facebook.com/SVidalBroker/
https://www.linkedin.com/in/sheilla-livewithdignity/
https://www.pinterest.com/SheillaVidal/
https://www.youtube.com/@livewithdignity9742/videos
https://www.instagram.com/sheillavidal/
Email: **sheilla.livewithdignity@gmail.com**
Phone: 707-653-0527
Website: **https://livewithdignity.mailchimpsites.com/**
Subscribe to my newsletter: **https://livewithdignity.mailchimpsites.com/newsletters**

MANIFESTING ABUNDANCE
BY ELLE BALLARD

My Cultural Background and Upbringing

I was born in the republic of Kazakhstan that was part of the USSR at the time; now it is a separate country. My childhood was a very happy childhood; my parents worked hard to provide for all four kids in the family. Both of my parents worked full-time jobs and then at *dacha* (an outside cottage in the suburb) where our family grew our own fruits and vegetables starting in the spring to the late summer months every year. They then sold some of the collected harvest at the local farmer's markets, and this provided additional, supplemental income for our family to afford a music school education for me and my sister, which my parents had to pay for. I still remember the joy I experienced when they delivered a brand-new piano to our door. A few kids from the neighborhood came to celebrate with me, and it was one of the highlights of my childhood. The USSR was an interesting place to live in. We did not have bottled water, sometimes not even such basic needs as toilet paper. Some houses did not even have refrigerators, so getting my own real piano delivered was a huge celebration for me as a child. I still remember that excitement.

I remember during the USSR collapse in 1991, there was a shortage of everything; it was hard to get things even if you had enough money to pay for it. You had to know the right people to be able to have access to some of the basic needs even such a necessity as warm blankets. People who you had to know were often people who occupied high-level positions or worked in the trading and sales industry where they had direct access to things not accessible to the average person. My aunt and my friend's mom used to work in the commerce industry and had access to acquire different things firsthand whereas average people did not have access to this. I remember wanting to work in that same industry myself so I could provide these things to myself and my family. This all changed when international borders started opening up, giving people a chance to travel the world, and I decided to enter the university and learn English. This in itself was a huge decision that influenced a lot of things in my personal and professional life.

Kazakhstan was always a Muslim country where women are first and foremost expected to get married and have children; they could have a career, but their family and kids should be a priority. A lot of women are highly educated, women capable of so much more in their lives, but society norms are usually heavy and something that people are expected to follow and not question. This was the reality for women in Kazakhstan, and the way the women are positioned. I am so happy to see how these beliefs are questioned today, and how more and more women are living happier lives and being able to make their life decisions based on their desires and wishes.

Manifesting My Dream Life

There was one other moment I vividly remember when me, my sister, and my cousin were sitting outside and dreaming out loud when we were thirteen years old. My younger sister was two years younger, and my cousin was the same year as I. Each one of us had to name the country we wanted to live in the future, I said, 'USA,' my sister said, 'Switzerland,' and my cousin said, 'oh well, I will live in the village.' This was at the time when our international borders were still closed, and we could not travel outside of the USSR.

About fourteen years later, after having built a successful career in my own country, I moved to the US and started building my life here. I completely forgot about this conversation with my sister and cousin until very recently... Everything we talked about came true. Our dreams can and do come true.

I had a brief experience of building my own business and fell in love with the freedom of creating anything I wanted, charging anything I wanted, and working the hours I wanted to work. I really wanted to create that life for me. I remember reading the book, *Young and Successful*, and learning so much from it. I also remember a round-table discussion during my MBA experience when we all shared what we wanted to do. The minute I shared I wanted to build a company, everyone cheered me on and shared the energetic vibrations they felt coming from me when I shared it. (This was another manifesting moment). But my doubts still occupied the majority of my brain, so I went ahead and finished an MBA program and found a job in a very multinational environment with the ability of learning and growing, I loved it. Isn't it funny how we can hold ourselves back and find excuses? After completing my MBA with a focus on marketing, I started working in the marketing capacity and loved the experience I was getting, but I was still dreaming of more. After a few years though, I still felt I was missing something and started thinking about launching my own company again. I had all the creative notes and ideas on any kind of products out there; this kept me so excited, but I still could not drop what I was doing.

A few years later, and after moving to another company where I again exercised myself in the international capacity, working in the international markets which I loved, my company got sold out and I, along with a few other colleagues, was let go.

I decided this was my time, and I made a decision not to look for another job but instead to go and start building the life that I wanted for me and the business that I had always dreamt of. I realized everything that had happened up until this point, had happened for a reason: my lessons, challenges, experience, and education.

My few entrepreneurial experiences gave me such a great practical experience of being in business for myself, something that we do not learn in an MBA program. Along with building my business, I started meeting so many amazing mentors and coaches who helped me grow and showed me the way. I am so thankful for them. I discovered a completely new world of entrepreneurship and successful women. And I loved this world.

Money and Our Self-Worth

I was very coachable and learning and grasping anything I could. I started learning about myself more and more, and one of the big lessons for me was that being in business is first and foremost a reflecting of my own side to myself, growing myself through this journey, and re-discovering myself every day. That is when I also started uncovering a lot of hidden beliefs about money that held me back; for example, that I had to work hard to make money. Some of the beliefs were formed because of my cultural upbringing, some of them were due to my own life experience. I realized that a lot of things I believed in are not true, and once I uncovered that, I had a lot of wonderful Aha moments. When I reclaimed my worthiness, and who I truly am, everything started falling into place.

Based on my own experience and the experiences of other women I talk to, our self-worth is closely connected to money. Our imposter syndrome comes in every time, and we might notice it when we try to increase our fees. Once I had that awareness, I was then able to work through it and uncover a lot of subconscious beliefs and obstacles that are no longer serving me. We all have that and it is important to work on those and give ourselves permission to live richer and prosperous lives.

Money and Abundance in Life

I love to talk about abundance in life and how that connects back to money, but also not only to money, but everything else in our lives. All of the areas of our life are interconnected-- money, energy, and all other areas.

I believe in full abundance in life; there is no limit. I do not believe in working ourselves to death to earn the money, but then living a miserable life and not being able to enjoy that money fully, however you define that enjoyment for yourself.

That is why I am passionate about helping multinational women reach full abundance in all areas of their life including business, health, relationships, spirituality, and passion. I also believe that there is a strong connection between our self-love, our worthiness, and money. Each one of us is so unique and amazing and each one of us always has something to bring to the table and until we fully tap into that, we cannot hear our own voice and feel our authenticity and how we are different and unique. There are so many ways to make money today, there are so many opportunities, it is important to find you in these voices; hear your voice, feel your passion, and then follow it with your heart. You will know you are on the right track because you will feel it with your heart.

Below are my five tips on creating more abundance in your life. Have fun in the journey of your life abundance and enjoy these tips:

Five Tips to Create More Abundance in Life

1. **Create a life manifesto or life mission** for yourself that includes your values and what you stand for.
   Whenever you face a question or challenge on how to continue moving forward or what to do, you can always refer to this manifesto and it will show you the way to move forward by bringing your focus to what matters to you and your big picture, thus shifting your attention from the issue in the moment and reminding you of your bigger 'why.'

2. **Be intentional and pay attention** to all areas of your life: Health, Relationships, Spirituality, Business/Profession.

In our Women of the World Network® community, we take time every year to plan for the next year, and we do that through allocating everything that we want to do and filtering it through all these areas of our life. We also filter it through our personal life mission that we talked about above. That way, you definitely do not miss out on anything in your life, but you are also able to drop something you do not need to be doing.

3. **Listen to your voice, wishes, and life hints.** Just like I said, 'I will live in the USA' without realizing any of it would happen, we can really create anything we want in life. And life does tell us what is good for us, we feel it. If you feel something brings you enormous joy, this is probably what you should be pursuing.

4. **Study your abundance beliefs and your self-worth beliefs.** What do they mean for you in your life? Very often, our money and overall life abundance connects to our self-worth and our belief in ourselves. I sometimes hear women say they are ready to pay others but not ready to charge for their own services. Women often have some hidden beliefs that we keep believing, and we do not know how to tell the difference or how to separate them or even if they are present at all. It could be cultural or upbringing beliefs that we possess; it could be fear, fear of success or fear of failure. Uncover what is holding you back and work on overcoming that and shift your belief in your thinking.

5. **Create a wish list for your life.** While working on the wish list, do not limit yourself based on your current financial or any life situation, think as if you had no limits and think really big because when you achieve that goal, you might ask yourself, "why did I not have a bigger goal?"

Living in abundance and time and money freedom is our birthright. I want to see every woman in this world achieve that for herself. I believe you can too and on your own terms.

Elle Ballard

Elle's successful marketing communication and product sales experience, coupled with her international business experience, makes her approach to business unique and powerful. She has been a featured guest on the following podcasts: "Expand Your Fempire," "The Art of Feminine Marketing," "Voice of America," and others.

Elle is an open-minded, conscious, global leader who is passionate about supporting multinational women in business and in life. Elle's attitude of abundance to life and business helps her clients get laser-focused on their mission and unique individual strengths to successfully build and promote their businesses, transform their lives, and gain freedom.

In her free time, Elle enjoys ballroom dancing, and traveling, and studies longevity and holistic health.

web: **www.elleballard.com**
web: **www.womenoftheworldnetwork.com**
IG: **https://www.instagram.com/theelleballard/**
FB: **https://www.facebook.com/theelleballard/**
LI: **https://www.linkedin.com/in/elviraballard/**

LIVING LIFE ON YOUR OWN TERMS

Gina,

Live your Best life!
Live your truth!

FINDING PURPOSE AND MEANING IN LIFE
BY MIRANTI OJONG

Early Beginnings

I was fortunate in the beginning of my life to have been blessed into a family that both valued faith, education, family, and culture and the tenacity to win in life. Like most families in early generations, things started with humble beginnings. In this case, my grandfather was the one to forever change the path of our family. Guided in faith and pure love for his family, specifically his mother, he sought peace, answers, and a way to help the greater good through words and information. One of his teachings, that's been passed down through the generations and I learned from my father, is to **follow your passion but also to be the best in that passion and field. Learn everything you can about it and live your life fully day by day in pursuit of greatness.**

As I learn from today's influencers, philosophers, coaches, mentors, humanitarians, and business leaders, I soon realized that what I learned and was told in my family would soon be very familiar and repeated in daily feeds and books.

To be successful was not guided by money. In fact, to reap the most rewards, you shouldn't even think about your own personal gains. You need to think about how what you do can really create value for others and really help solve a genuine problem and need. It was only when I learned this and to live a life of servitude, both in the non-profit and profitable worlds, that I really understood the meaning of living a fulfilling life and a life full of purpose.

While this book is about finance, it's not meant to be a how-to. You can Google that. Watch YouTube. Attend workshops and seminars. Confide in a trusted advisor and friend. No, it's meant to be a how can you think, how can you change the way you think, how can you perceive things differently, how can you value that which is the most pertinent in your life to live a truly wealthy happy life.

Early Teachings and Values

I was taught to truly maximize the value of the dollar that you spend. Ten-dollar items were scoffed at in our family early in my childhood, not because we were too good for it, but because my father also taught me that you need to buy quality. **Spend more on the front end on quality, and you will be happy using it for years and decades to come.** Did you know I still have a wool bomber jacket that my mother wore while she was pregnant with me in Germany? Classic style, quality material, and passed down the generations. Now you might not like the idea of hand-me-downs, but that's beside the point. Are you buying a leather purse or pleather? And I get it, you might not be able to afford such things, but could you save and hold yourself for just a few more months so you can afford a higher quality and end up wearing with pride? Not to mention, if you do end up getting bored with it, it's resale value is much higher on those online merchant portals. Am I right? Or am I right?

But this talk isn't meant to be about bags and material things. It's a way of thinking. It's a mindset. It's what you value. It's what you take care of in life. It's what will ultimately make you happy and wealthy, and I'm not solely talking about money. The real truth is that you're living your life and going through a journey of self-discovery.

Life Lessons

I can tell you that I've had the fancy shoes, designer handbags, driven the luxury cars, dined in Michelin Star restaurants, flown international business class, built chateaus, and the list goes on.... But you meet me today? I'm in search for the ultimate minimalist lifestyle. Seeking advice from many business coaches, mentors, obsessively researching about van-life, and even finding enlightenment through KonMari. Throughout my life, ever since I shared with my father in the backseat of the car coming home from high school at sixteen years old. I will find a business that will give me passive income, the freedom to decide how to spend my time, and it will be simple tasks and easy systems. One that grants me the freedom to roam this country, take a break when I want, dine where I want, and anything else with intention. My father just laughed and said no such thing. Challenge accepted. From that point on, especially after my baby brother, Michael Stephen, passed away that same year, I vowed to live life to the fullest. Experience everything once and then have a valid opinion. He was only able to live for five days, but I promised I would live life fully for him. Do what he would be missing. And with that mentality and gumption to seize every moment I live, I was able to experience a multitude of things that one would still dream of.

After elementary school, which I didn't have much choice in attending, I knew I had to take control of the decision I had for high school. I didn't follow the crowd. No magnet schools, not the typical applications sent. In fact, I begged for a boarding school, to no avail. So instead, I chose one of the most prestigious single-sex high schools in the nation, Convent of the Sacred Heart San Francisco, where I would learn to be empowered as a female. Where it doesn't matter what gender you are, you make sure you are qualified, and you can work the hardest and smartest to get the best results.

I even worked my way to acceptance at Cornell University's Hotel School, the best in the industry in the world. Networked my way in, something they inevitably taught there too. Sought after internships that meant getting rejected from hourly local pizza joints to then negotiating a program at the number one high-end luxury hotel in the city. Yes, the universe has a funny way of steering you through the course of your intended life for a reason.

It wasn't enough that I earned my way to an Ivy League, having perfected English, my third language of six. This is coming from even knowing a single word at age six when I moved to the US. I graduated cum laude. And not only that but I really learned what is necessary to do well in this industry that I had a passion for because of my grandfather's pioneering. From then on, it was taking more advanced master's classes, getting the best industry internships, and then landing the only reputable job available post 9/11 amidst so many qualified classmates. Yup, the universe is funny again, right? And after two years of living independently as a young, first-time homeowner in Washington, DC and helping manage twenty-five full-service hotels across the country, I knew I had to start my own business. No matter what information I had gained in school and corporate jobs, the only path to financial freedom was to own a business with a well-run proven system. And yet, I still kept searching and searching for this.

Transitions

I moved back to the SF Bay Area after two years of learning from the best asset managers. I took an opportunity to work on a new project in the wine country. It was a dream come true since I had been obsessed with construction and developing from as far back as I can remember. In fact, I can show you pictures when I was four years old playing with a piece of 2 x 4 and dirt on my father's construction site. Environment and associations really do have a way of shaping you and encouraging your newfound passions.

While I managed this project and eventually earned my general contractor's license, I knew that I had to learn more about everything. Fortunately, I had some friends in the tech space, so we started companies, founded non-profit hackathons for the physically challenged, pioneered my own e-commerce space, and really just had a thirst for how things and companies worked. All the while I was involved with my alma mater and led our local chapter as president for many years and eventually led the entire Pacific Northwest and Hawaii Region as RVP. Serving on nonprofit boards across industries and understanding top-down strategies really guided the next few years. I even agreed to work at Facebook on a special project that would benefit from my hospitality expertise.

Some personal misdirection occurred during this time, and without going into much detail, I knew I needed to add another kind of business that didn't have me at the job site from the crack of dawn to sometimes unknown hours. Physically, I was tired, and I knew I definitely didn't have the answer yet to what I had been seeking since the backseat conversations with my father. So, I decided to be a contract worker, Instacart to be exact. While I do not encourage such career paths long term, it was one of the most humbling experiences I needed to learn when things didn't quite go my way. After two months of that full-time, enough was enough, so I started yet another e-commerce company. I didn't even publicize this too much because it was so far off my usual passions. But I thought, I can't imagine people not being happy looking at beautiful exotic flowers... problem here was that I had invested in a seasonal and perishable business. Not a good plan for a year-round consistent business.

But I am blessed and fortunate to have come across that business that's given me the opportunity to fulfill my big dreams and really see that it's within reach. And it only took one graduation day, a folding table, a self-printed logo, a five-minute conversation, and then a life-changing appointment that would steer me away from that recent real estate license I had passed and a subpar business plan. From that moment on, I would challenge everything I knew about business, about school, about how life really worked through the many seminars, team coachings, mentorship, and helping those less fortunate as a licensed insurance professional. Everything I learned and realized, I was never taught those things that would reach personal financial freedom and to fully realize the American "retirement."

Of course, it will not be easy, but hard work does pay off, and sacrifice is always essential to growth or whatever it is you seek. Remember, temporary sacrifices are needed for long-term fulfillment and achievement of life-long goals. I, too, need to remind myself of this every day, but that is the fun of it. That is the true power of finding financial freedom. It's not necessarily about the dollar amount, but what you need to be really happy in your life and to fund your lifestyle.

And this is the beautiful thing, I haven't figured it all out yet. I don't have all the pieces up to this point. And notice I mention "yet" several times in this chapter. Remember that if you are not living your best life, you still have yet to do what's necessary to accomplish that. It might be today, it might be tomorrow, it might be a month from now, and for others, years, but just be intentional in what you are doing and that you are going at your own pace in your own life.

Ongoing Pursuit in Life

I believe that I have a choice and I am not stuck or struggling with something that I have no control over. The thing is that I have every control right now, to do everything, and I am more and more determined to try to move that needle. Am I supposed to be contributing to a bigger impact, I know I impact people every day, but is there something bigger than that? I am very mindful of, "why am I doing this? How am I because of this?"

That was the whole point. I'd like to transcend into something different. **To elevate, to go through whatever life gives to you, because to do something very impactful to thousands, tens of thousands, millions of people, it's not going to take normal thinking, it's going to take a very different kind of mindset, and perhaps it's one that hasn't been thought of**

before. While there is clarity in what is important, such as faith, family, and freedom, it's the specific purpose that we are in search of. What value do we place on money? What value do we place on freedom? What value do we place on time? Whatever background or experiences you have, whatever environment you're in, whatever circumstances you've helped to shape, the answer becomes clearer through each journey, through each meaningful purpose, so that a new, clearer definition reveals itself as you peel off the layers. **Life is yours. You live it. You create it. You define it.**

Miranti Ojong

Miranti Ojong is a serial entrepreneur. She is a licensed California General Building Contractor and a licensed California Realtor. Currently, she is a financial services agency builder, has her insurance license in nineteen states and continues to expand across the US, where she financially educates clients and business owners in various demographics and communities. Her services include retirement planning, investments, life, health and disability insurance, estate planning, college planning, and business financial planning. She is a mentor and trainer to agents and independent business owners in her profession to help guide their success and reach their life and career goals. Her mission is to empower every individual with the right knowledge and tools to achieve financial independence.

Miranti, a German-born Indonesian, grew up in San Francisco since she was six years old. As a native San Franciscan who attended St. Stephen's Catholic School and Convent of the Sacred Heart HS, she continues to be involved with the alumni and parish of these schools. After attending Cornell University's School of Hospitality Administration with a concentration in real estate development for her undergrad, she returned to San Francisco to be with her family and to expand their real estate portfolio. She continues to guide Cornell Hotel Society Chapter leaders in the Pacific

Northwest and Hawaii region and to strengthen alumni involvement. When she's not helping to protect and grow families' assets, she is also managing her hospitality business in Sonoma Wine Country. She enjoys spending all her free time with family, seeking adventures in the outdoors and unknown terrain, and being one with nature for inspiration, relaxation, and peace.

Facebook: **https://www.facebook.com/mirantiusa**
Instagram: **@miranti.o**
https://www.linkedin.com/in/miranti/
Miranti Ojong
info@mirantillc.com

Dear Gina,
Here's to your dreams
coming true!
Alpana

MY AMERICAN DREAM:
FROM IMMIGRANT TO ENTREPRENEUR
BY ALPANA ARAS-KING

Have you ever had a dream that seemed impossible?

As an immigrant who came to this country with nothing, I want to take you on a journey through my entrepreneurial story to inspire you to tap into your own potential and to go after your dreams–whether it is to generate an income, make an impact, or become an influential figure.

My journey to be bold and be seen.

I came to America in search of my freedom and the American Dream.

I had two suitcases, a thousand dollars, my mom's pressure cooker, and a handwritten recipe book.

Someone told me to get a boyfriend, a car, and work in a coffee shop.

Those didn't happen for me quickly, nor did I ever get to fulfill my dream of working in a coffee shop.

I began my career as a family photographer, which grew into a decade-long, commercial career working with multinational companies, traveling internationally to help nonprofits, and helping women entrepreneurs with personal branding.

Today, I am a Visual Brand Coach, Storyteller, and International Photographer with work published by *The NY Times*, Apple, and Instagram.

I have several passive income streams, including stock photography and a cookbook, and I plan to open an online store and create a visibility show.

My mission is to help purpose-driven women entrepreneurs embody their brand story to stand out, get visible, make an impact, and create wealth.

Over the years, my triumphs and heartaches have taught me so much, about myself and others.

I still have a lot to accomplish, and so do you, but let's take a moment to celebrate how far we've come as women from where our stories began.

Early Days in India

I was born a city girl in the bustling city of Bombay, India.

There is an unsaid expectation for every middle-class Indian to get a college education, save money, and marry a partner picked by their parents.

I have always been a rebel.

The black sheep of the family marching to my own drum.

Somewhere deep down, I felt a desire to chart my own course in life–a life different from my mother's and women in my country who didn't have a voice or get seen.

After my BFA in design, I marched right into the world of marketing and advertising, which opened me up to new possibilities.

My father, an entrepreneur and risk-taker, quit a secure job to start his own business while my mother stayed home to raise my two siblings and me. He was frugal, but he believed in purchasing quality products that would last and cared about aesthetics. My father was also a savvy investor and purchased real estate that were "vacation homes" within a few hours driving distance from Bombay.

My mother, a college-educated woman, was the super mom who cared for us, helped with homework, and cooked wholesome meals for the family.

I can still recall the smell of my mother's freshly cooked mutton curry wafting through the house on Sundays. The sound of the *vatis* (small containers) scraping against plates filled me with anticipation as I waited for hot *phulkas* (bread) to eat with the mutton curry at the dinner table with my siblings.

But growing up, seeing gender inequality, with different rules for men and women, didn't sit well with me, as I saw my mother's place was clearly defined as less important than my father's and she was without a voice.

Women didn't have a say in financial matters, and most, like my mother, didn't make an income, which made me determined to change things for myself. However, the lack of female role models or financial education made it difficult as it wasn't a topic for discussion.

My inner rebel was my guiding star.

I've been a hustler since I was a kid.

We had to do a fundraising drive in elementary school through "Brick Cards." While there was no personal financial incentive, I took it on as a challenge, perhaps due to the possibility of winning a small prize.

After exhausting efforts to get my parents, aunts, and uncles to donate, I took to the streets. I'd stop random strangers by the bus stop.

"Sir/Madam, would you like to donate a rupee (about twenty cents) to my school building fund?" I'd ask, fluttering my big hazel eyes.

Some passersby took pity on me and said 'yes'; others didn't bother to answer. I learned how to handle rejection.

If there is one thing I want you to take away from this experience, it is to be okay with rejection. It served me well while pounding the pavement as an artist looking for work and later as an entrepreneur.

While I learned to hustle, I also had limiting beliefs about money rooted in my subconscious from media, culture, and family.

Like that popular Abba song –

"Money, money, money
I work all night,
I work all day to pay the bills I have to pay
Ain't it sad?"

We've all heard phrases like "Money doesn't grow on trees," and for most of us, those words led to the belief that money was scarce, and that it could run out.

Through the past several years of deep inner work, I have become aware of my conditioning and have consistently worked to shift my mindset and, most importantly, to not pass it on to my son.

Green Card

When I got admitted to Clarion University for my master's program in instructional design, I felt like I had won the lottery.

I got a tuition waiver and $1500/year as financial aid. It wasn't a lot of money to live on, but I knew I had to make it work.

I lived in a house with international students where the rent was cheap. One of my housemates—a Chinese man—would get up in the mornings singing songs at five a.m., which was my alarm. He routinely hung his tighty-whities in the shared bathroom on a hanger.

In college, I survived on comfort food of rice and dal (lentils) that I cooked in my mom's pressure cooker. On occasion, I splurged on cheap American food while working a second job washing dishes in the school cafeteria. My upbringing of saving money and living within my means came in handy, not just because it helped me graduate debt-free from college, but also because it prepared me well for the future.

When I graduated, the recession hit, and I had to find a job quickly. When you aren't an engineer, finding a job, let alone a green card sponsor, was next to impossible. Finally, a small direct marketing company in Peoria offered me a job as a graphic designer for $26,000. I realized I needed to get a driver's license (and learn to drive). I passed the test on my third attempt using a random student's borrowed car, and I bought a used Toyota Corolla for $4,000. My sister drove me to Peoria, where I spent the next two and a half years overworked and underpaid.

My green card brought me the freedom to move to a bigger city.

WOMEN MONEY, AND INFLUENCE

My Investment Made Over Half a Million Dollars

It was love at sight when I visited San Francisco for the first time.

It was like that love song "I Left My Heart In San Francisco" by Tony Bennett playing in my head.

As an immigrant with wanderlust, I finally put down roots in a city. I've been through many seasons of life here and grew into my own as an entrepreneur.

I moved to the city for my second master's in computer art, draining my savings and taking on some debt. I hated my college program, dropped out, and took up freelance work. This was before the Internet era, and I would walk into offices confidently to drop off my resumé and, on occasion, get an interview with the hiring manager as I hustled to get work.

Two years later, in 1998, my now-husband Kip followed me to move into my one-bedroom apartment in lower Nob Hill. He didn't have a job and had around $36,000 in student loans, some in default from late payments and credit card debt. This shocked my nervous system as someone who had a relatively debt-free life.

We spent money frugally, on rent and food. Our one luxury was a mile-away parking spot for $75 instead of five times that for one downtown. Of course, it meant having to walk home with a sack of potatoes rather than getting the car out.

I cooked meals at home, and we ate out on occasion. One of my local favorites was Shalimar, a cheap Pakistani restaurant that bordered the sketchy tenderloin to get chicken tikka masala and bhuna ghost with naan. It had no ambiance, which reminded me of the local *dhabas* (roadside eateries) back in India, but the food always hit the spot. Or we'd stand in line to get delicious Chinese food at the House of Nanking, where the no-nonsense

68

owner had no time for pleasantries. We'd laugh about how quickly they wanted payment and walk away full but slightly frazzled after every visit.

My boyfriend got a great job offer at a hospital in a few months, and we kept our frugal lifestyle.

I took over managing the finances, and he made the maximum payments possible to pay his loans. I took advantage of 0 percent credit cards, transferring from one to another every six months or so as a strategy to pay off my small school debt.

In two years, my husband paid off his entire debt with my help—the subsidized Stafford, Perkins, HPSL/PCL loans, and a couple of grants/waivers.

I got my dream job as Principal Designer at Headland, an interactive web agency where I got paid well as a contractor. I got offered a full-time job where I made close to $100,000, the highest I earned at an artist's job.

It was a moment that I can't even describe.

I was no longer a starving artist.

I worked with clients like Penguin Books, Rough Guides, and Financial Times, all early adopters of the dot-com boom. I managed the launch of the Lifelong Learning website, partnering with tech leads and producers to create style guides, functionality, and navigation.

Since I finally had money to invest, I opened my first investment account with TD Waterhouse.

This is where I want you to consider your money mindset when investing like me.

How do you feel about saving vs losing money when there are no guarantees?

For me, it felt scary but exciting too. At the back of my mind was that little voice, that reminded me of the women in my family who didn't have the opportunity like I did or their own money.

I spent inordinate amounts of time researching stocks through The Motley Fool and creating mock portfolios before taking the plunge into buying stocks and mutual funds.

I bought stocks like Cisco, Intel, eBay, and Home Depot. Some lost money and others did well.

I convinced my husband to get an IRA account like mine. I helped him invest, and one of my stock purchases—Apple—yielded over half a million dollars. If you'd told my younger self what I could do, I would have laughed at you for being crazy.

The Birth of Storyboxart

In 2003, I gave birth to my son Rowan and became a stay-at-home mom.

Motherhood shifted my perspective and I found that the idyllic "American Dream" was slipping further away.

While I loved my son more than life, something inside me felt restless as I thought of my mother and her invisibility.

In 2006, while at home with my son, a woman came to purchase a baby carrier I had listed on Craigslist. She also saw my framed photos from the Himalayas and asked if I would photograph her baby. That was my first paid client and the start of Storyboxart, which became a successful photography business.

It was scary to charge more than my "competition," although, in reality, I didn't get into the comparison game as I wanted a sustainable business.

I recall how soul-crushing it was when a potential client in my early days would say, "You are so expensive."

I hated sales calls.

If you have struggled with this or any other business area, know that you are not alone.

My advice is to find the gaps where you need support for your business and invest in mentors who can fast-track your learning. Over the years, I have invested five figures by hiring one-to-one coaches, joining mastermind groups, and buying a gazillion courses to help me strengthen my mindset, marketing efforts, writing skills, leadership skills, and more. You simply cannot do it without the right support.

I have learned I am the right person for the right people.

We prioritize things we value and are ready to spend on them.

Recently after a photo session, I was talking to my client, Paula.

She's been a client of mine for over a decade and is also a friend.

"I don't drive a fancy car but value my investment in your work."

And then she pointed to her modest vehicle.

WOMEN, MONEY, AND INFLUENCE

"I look at pictures Alpana has taken of Jamey and remember her as she was then.

I hope that when I am not around that she will be able to look at the pictures of us and remember how we were, how much she is, and was loved."

Women are unsung heroes.

We juggle careers, family, and social commitments without making space for our own dreams.

We sacrifice ourselves for others and wear a mask of perfection that hides our true identity.

But it's time to stop hiding in plain sight and step into the light—to find our true selves and create a life that feels authentic.

Be Bold. Be Seen.

Coming to America was a leap of faith in myself.

After working intimately with women, I have seen how fearful they are of being seen. It has paralleled my journey as a badass photographer behind the camera and not in front of it.

It prompted me to step into my discomfort in 2019 to create the PowHer Up show, where I interviewed twenty-one experts in mindset, social media, and finance to help women entrepreneurs uplevel their businesses.

Stepping into that bolder version of myself helped me pivot my photography business, which came to a standstill in the COVID-19 pandemic, and helped me help women in their transformation. Now I empower women entrepreneurs to step into their brands boldly and unapologetically through one-to-one coaching and storytelling photo sessions.

As I close out this chapter, I want to share five things that can help you.

Know your WHY. The more you know who you are and what you stand for, the better able you'll be to make money doing what makes you happy. Simon Sinek's TED talk is one of the most popular videos on YouTube. In it, he provides a framework for finding your why—the reason you do what you do.

Build a business, not a hobby. If you don't charge sustainably, you may be energetically deflated. Consider product and labor costs, along with operating and marketing expenses for your business. My company has expenses like CRM software, website, social media, copy tools, marketing, web developers, virtual assistants, designers, studio equipment, and gear that factor into my pricing. When I launched a new product, I started with a low-price offer, which is now a high-ticket offer at ten times the price.

Celebrate your wins, whether small or large, personal or professional. For me, one of the biggest celebrations has been raising a wonderful nineteen-year-old who is studying data science in college while holding a part-time job, and helping him set up an IRA.

Invest in your personal brand. This will help you dig deeper into who you are, know your values, and magnetize your clients. It can be a platform for your expansion as you grow and create new offerings. Last year, I launched a storytelling cookbook as a tribute to my mother and sold fifty copies to my followers through my list and social media.

Be Bold. Be Seen. My journey from immigrant to entrepreneur was my quest to be seen. I'm here to tell you: You deserve to be seen. Because if I could do it, so can you! **Every single woman deserves to be seen,** including you!

Alpana Aras-King

Women entrepreneurs and purpose-driven leaders hire Alpana to grow their brand's visibility by unleashing their inner star power. Alpana of **alpanaaras.com** is a visual brand coach, international photographer, and storyteller, who combines strategic coaching with creative storytelling to create an irresistible personal brand to be bold and be seen for impact and influence.

From the glimmering heights of Indian ad agencies to US corporate offices, she has explored many career paths and been featured across some of the globe's top publications, including *The New York Times*, Instagram, and Apple Computers.

Alpana is passionate about helping women achieve success in business. She hosted an online summit called PowHer Up featuring twenty-one inspiring experts. She offers one-to-one coaching and offers online courses combined with unique storytelling sessions.

As an immigrant and person of color, Alpana harnesses the power of storytelling to promote diversity, inclusion, equity, and belonging. She leads a collective that uses visual storytelling as a tool through @everydaybayarea to tell impactful stories about diverse representation and to foster connections between people all over the world.

Connect with Alpana

https://linktr.ee/alpana.aras
Craft an Unforgettable Brand: Download Your FREE Guide
https://alpanaaras.com/5-key-elements-for-crafting-a-storytelling-brand/
Tips for Cultivating a Positive Money Mindset: Download Your FREE Guide
https://alpanaaras.com/money-mindset/
Website: https://alpanaaras.com/

LIVE THE LIFE YOU LOVE AS AN ENTREPRENEUR!
BY FAYE CALANGIAN

Paycheck to Paycheck

When I was a kid, my family struggled financially. I grew up in a family where only one parent worked, and we only had one income stream. That meant we were always living paycheck to paycheck, and sometimes money was tight. I remember my parents being stressed about our financial situation. They worried about paying the bills, ensuring we had enough food to eat, and covering our basic needs.

A Volcano Erupted without Warning in 1991

On June 15, 1991, when Mt. Pinatubo erupted, I was only nine years old. That was the day our world changed. A volcanic eruption in the Philippines caused a massive amount of sulfur dioxide to be released into the atmosphere, which spread across Asia. The effects were devastating. I remember seeing people wearing masks outside and hearing about how many children were getting sick because they had breathed in too much air pollution.

Unfortunately, I was one of those children who got sick due to air pollution. I remember waking up one morning with a sore throat and feeling like there was a heavy weight on my chest. My parents took me to the doctor, who diagnosed me with bronchitis, which led to pneumonia. The next few days, weeks, and months were spent in bed, recovering from a lung infection that I had developed due to breathing in too much ash.

At the same time, my father also lost his job because of the economic downturn that followed the eruption. With no work in the Philippines and with a sick child, my father decided to try his luck and find work elsewhere. He found a job as a construction worker in Guam. Nine years later, I moved with my siblings to live with him.

Life-Altering Experience

Living in a foreign country taught us many things, especially how to work hard and value money. I learned to appreciate the things my parents did for us, how one stream of income is not enough to support a family, and that it is important to have a backup plan. Learning how to be successful in this experience prepared me for later success.

I came to Guam, which is a US territory, with a dream of working hard, getting a good job, and making my family proud. I always wanted to finish my college education, but I didn't want to have a school loan, so I decided to move back and forth from Guam to Philippines until I completed my degree in bachelor of science in computer science in 2004. After graduating from college in the Philippines, I decided to move to San Francisco and find a job there.

Living in San Francisco in My Early Twenties

Living in San Francisco in my early twenties had some ups and downs. Because my degree was from the Philippines, finding a job was never easy. I worked full time in a small office in downtown San Francisco as clerk, while working part-time at a restaurant during the weekend. In between these jobs, I worked on getting my certification in web and graphic design. My English was still not perfect, but I was able to communicate with my coworkers and customers. I've always felt intimidated about that time, trying to communicate, because I couldn't speak English well. But I learned that, if you really want to do something, you can find a way. If you're willing to work hard, people will be more open to helping you out.

Without Hard Work, Luck Doesn't Happen

I started out as a project coordinator, but through diligence, hard work, and dedication, I was able to rise through the ranks until I eventually became a project manager.

As a project manager, I learn a lot about how to manage large projects, how to keep track of all the moving pieces, and how to coordinate with teams both inside and outside my company.

Although I was happy with my career then and now, working in a cubicle from nine to five made me feel like something was missing from my life. I wanted to make an impact in my community. Something that would give me a sense of purpose and meaning in my life.

I've always dreamed of running my own business, earning multiple sources of income, and helping other people through my experience.

I want to become a coach, a mentor, a teacher, and an entrepreneur.

My Biggest Supporter

I've always wanted to be an entrepreneur, but when I first started dreaming about it, I never imagined that I'd be able to make it happen. I mean, who does?

But then my husband came along and showed me that anything is possible if you just keep at it—and that's when things really started to click. He encouraged me to dream bigger and helped me understand the importance of never giving up on your dreams. Eventually, he even joined me in the journey by helping me start our own digital marketing company.

Without him, I would never have discovered that it was possible to be a coach, entrepreneur, and project manager at the same time.

Create Share Educate LLC Was Born

In January 2020, Create Share Educate LLC was born. Today, our goal is to help more and more small businesses and entrepreneurs grow their business online by providing them with the tools and resources they need to succeed. We do this through coaching programs, group training courses, webinars, and workshops as well as one-on-one consulting sessions.

In August 2020, I launched our signature program, **Build Together**, that focuses on teaching entrepreneurs how to build their own lead-generation machine using our proven strategies. We're a small but mighty team that consists of entrepreneurs and digital marketing specialists who are passionate about helping small businesses grow their online presence. We believe that the best way to get results is by providing our members with real, actionable advice and practical tools. We focus on teaching them how to build their own lead-generation machine using strategies that have been proven to work.

What was just an idea of helping my fellow nine-to-fivers with not just one income stream became a reality. I am so grateful for this opportunity, and every day I wake up with a smile on my face because I know that this is where I am supposed to be.

I still work as a project manager and my husband still works as an ICU nurse, but we worked our business around our lifestyles and schedules. We have been able to start a family, travel the world, and enjoy life while growing our businesses. We have also been able to help others achieve the same success and freedom through our training programs. Our goal is for everyone who joins us on this journey to be able to live their best life while doing what they love!

My Parents Legacy

I will never forget what my parents taught me: "**kapag may itinanim may aanihin.**" (Translation: If you plant seeds today, tomorrow there will be fruit). I have learned that the key to success is not just being smart but being committed and consistent with what you do. If you want to achieve your goals, don't give up on them, because they are worth it! I was once like anyone else, struggling to make ends meet. It wasn't until I finally learned how to generate multiple streams of income that I was able to start living the life I always wanted.

I wanted to help entrepreneurs like me who want to build a business while working full time. Therefore, I created an online community for entrepreneurs who are just starting a business, have built one while working full time or part-time, or are trying to build a portfolio of businesses while maintaining a day job, to understand the potential of their business and identify growth opportunities but don't have the time or resources (like me). The community is called Create Share Educate for Entrepreneurs, and it's a place where entrepreneurs can get support from other like-minded people, learn from my team and me, and build an online business that works for them. We are a community of men and women entrepreneurs who want to create more freedom in their lives. We offer online classes, live events, and coaching as well as access to some of my best resources at no cost. I want entrepreneurs around the world to experience what it feels like when you finally say 'yes' to yourself and all the things you've been dreaming about doing.

The Create Share Educate Community

I started with nothing but a vision and a laptop. I spent nights and weekends learning how to build an online business. I have been fortunate to build a successful business on my own terms, but it wasn't easy. I have spent many hours learning from my mistakes, and it has taken me over a year to figure out what works and what doesn't. When I started learning all the ropes in building a successful business, I told myself there maybe others who also need that support in starting a business.

This is why I created the Create Share Educate Community to support aspiring entrepreneurs in their process and journey when starting a business. What I share in the community is a simplified marketing process and proven tools to help entrepreneurs succeed and not give up in the early stage of their business (even while working full-time or part-time)

I want aspiring entrepreneurs to have the opportunity to learn from my experiences, so they don't waste as much time trying different ideas that don't work. My mantra in building a business is, "build a business without sacrificing personal or family time." I want aspiring entrepreneurs to know that they can do it too.

The community is just one way I want to help people build lives they love through entrepreneurship. I now wake up in the morning with so much gratefulness in my heart knowing that I am making an impact in the life of my community every day.

Supporting aspiring entrepreneurs built their dream business while working full time or part-time is my ongoing mission.

Faye Calangian

Faye Calangian is a project manager and founder of Create Share Educate LLC for Entrepreneurs where she helps hybrid entrepreneurs (coaches, consultants, and service providers) create a system on How to Go From Four to Five Figures consistently. She has a step-by-step program called Build Together Lab, focusing on system and project management, that shows you exactly how to consistently sign clients no matter where you are.

Faye teaches entrepreneurs tools on how to create quality content and help devise a simple content marketing plan or strategy to stay consistent. She coaches entrepreneurs on navigating Facebook and Instagram to create traffic and ten times this traffic for more business. She educates entrepreneurs on the action steps for building an email list and creates courses to teach different online marketing strategies.

Faye believes that having multiple streams of income is the key to financial freedom and early retirement. Faye has been able to help dozens of entrepreneurs build a system for their business to transition from a nine to five job into a business that makes an extra income for them and their families. Faye was born and raised in the Philippines, but she moved to the US when she was sixteen years old. She studied bachelor of science at a Philippines university. and worked as a project manager before deciding that she wanted to make a change in her life. Faye launched her own small business with just $100, and within six months, she had already generated over $40,000 in revenue. Her mistakes—and successes—have helped shape who she is as an entrepreneur; now Faye can help others grow their businesses too.

Social Media Accounts

web: **www.sheispower.club**
Instagram: **www.instagram.com/felisafayeblog**
Facebook business page: **https://www.facebook.com/createshareeducate forentrepreneurs**
LinkedIn: **https://www.linkedin.com/in/createshareeducatellc/**
Facebook Community: **https://www.facebook.com/groups/teamcreate-shareeducate**
Email: **fcalangian@gmail.com**

WHAT'S SELF-WORTH GOT TO DO WITH IT?
BY MARY ANN FAREMOUTH

There is a famous quote by Henry David Thoreau that has always resonated with me. He wrote, "There is no value in life except what you choose to place upon it and no happiness in any place except what you bring to it yourself."

As an executive recruiter for over thirty years, I am amazed at how our self-worth plays such an important role in our ability to make a living. There is power in realizing that the way you think of yourself and treat yourself creates the foundation for how others will think of you and treat you.

In an article from *Forbes* magazine, writer Ashley Stahl cites a medical study that estimates that **85 percent of the world's population experiences low self-esteem**. The causes for this statistic are undoubtedly complex, but in the business world, we see the effects of it on a regular basis.

Stahl writes, "Low self-esteem and a low sense of self-worth not only negatively affect our personal growth, they also cripple our professional prospects. My experience has shown time and time again that people with higher self-worth have higher salaries. Self-esteem may even affect your salary as much as cognitive abilities do. It's the subjective internal measure that you place on yourself. Confident people landed the job because they perceived themselves in a positive light and they exuded confidence."

I believe we work to build the self-esteem and confidence we need to also reach for that higher salary. I have seen that the quest for a higher salary might be more challenging for women, especially those subjected to generations of gendered stereotypes, suggesting that women should be a bit more reserved and passive than our male counterparts. But the world is changing rapidly, and in the new work world, women can be less afraid these days to demand their true value. In fact, I believe it is critical that we hold our value highly and should expect a fair and right salary.

I remember dealing with a very difficult plant manager in another state who was referred to me by the corporate office VP where I had made many placements. When I called him, he told me he didn't want to work with me because I was a woman and not an engineer. After taking a deep breath, I told him that I would be happy to fly out to his plant on my dime (my expense), let him meet me, and decide if I could fill his jobs. Well, that year I filled twenty-eight of his plant jobs. If I had not had strong self-worth and the determination to succeed, I might not have been able to report this story of success. I was willing to invest in myself and believed in myself enough to stand up for myself.

These vital abilities, to perceive yourself clearly and positively, to cultivate a durable and grounded sense of confidence in your skills and abilities, and to feel pride in the value that you bring to your employer, are the qualities that can help you achieve your professional goals.

So how do we balance these qualities? How do we develop this healthier sense of self while still manifesting humility and respect? If we truly are the captains of our own ships and the ones driving the boats, how can we determine our own value instead of leaving it up to others? I believe the answer has a lot to do with how we learn from our experiences and how we cultivate our mindset.

Here are some of the tools and teachings I use as a professional recruiter and consultant to support my clients in elevating their sense of self-worth and therefore strengthening their ability to make a good living. Translate each of these suggestions to make them work in the unique circumstances of your own life and your own career. Hopefully these practices will help you delete those old tapes of self-doubt and allow you to move forward into a brighter mindset that will result in a stronger sense of your own innate value. And who knows, they might even lead you to a better job offer!

Claim Your Self-Worth:

1. Remind Yourself That You Are Worthy

Worthiness does not mean entitlement. Meador Devor, author of *The Worthy Project* writes, "Worthiness is the quality of deserving attention, energy, and respect. It's not confidence. It's not bravado. You can't fake worthiness, nor can you accidentally end up with it. Worthiness is like a muscle. There are things you can do to strengthen that muscle and there are plenty of things that will weaken it."

Start out each day with this positive mindset and strong determination to expand your personal and professional platform. Stop replaying those messages in your head over and over about how you didn't pass the CPA exam the first time around, or how working full-time and going to school at night took you longer than four years to get your degree. What is that really doing to your self-worth? Why not flip that negative self-talk into something like: "I'm pleased that I was able to not neglect my family while trying to pass the CPA test the first time," etc., or "It's great that I had the experience of working as well as going to school to bring my prospective employer more concrete skills that are not learned only in a classroom." When we focus on our own self-worth, our own deep worthiness, we focus on what we need and what we can offer to others. We let go of self-doubt. When we do this, we are driven by an inner compass that doesn't depend on external forces to validate our success.

2. Don't Be Afraid of Failure

We may not always understand at the time how a difficult challenge may turn out to be a real benefit to us later. A famous commencement address was given at Harvard a few years back by J.K. Rowling, the well-known author of the Harry Potter series. The address was titled, "The Benefits of Failure." I remember listening to that speech and hearing Ms. Rowling asked why she would stand up in front of a group of graduates of Harvard, who, to that point, probably had not failed that much, and talk about the benefits of failure? She then described details of her own life and how the many failures she had experienced were strong turning points that led her to her ability to believe in her own creativity and to create commercial success in her career.

Everyone fails. Even the most wildly successful, genius CEO only gained their seat by failing and learning from what went wrong. Recast your failures as turning points, as opportunities to see exactly what didn't work, and learn from them so that your next attempt is more successful.

3. Dress for the Job You Want, not Just the One You Have

Sure, we all wish we could go to work in comfortable attire, and the work-at-home days of the COVID-19 pandemic lockdown saw a lot of professionals working online in whatever they happened to be wearing. But I've had many clients and business owners complain to me lately, with online interviews being so common, that the candidate's attire in an interview was way too casual for the position they wanted to be hired for. I'm not suggesting that every job will require fully suited attire, but a professional look will never hurt you in an interview, and being overdressed as opposed to underdressed probably will never result in a negative result. What you wear reflects how seriously you take yourself and how seriously you would like others to take you.

For example, if being with a top firm in your industry is a big priority for you and you've been with a small, privately held firm for many years, would dressing in a more professional manner set the tone for you to feel more confident and demonstrate your personal value to that prospective employer? A professional look sets the tone for how you will be valued and how you will be treated.

4. Avoid an All-or-Nothing Attitude

If the last interview you went on did not result in getting an offer, don't fold your hands and decide to just stay where you are. Talk to a trusted friend or a professional consultant about how the interview went and get some clear feedback about what you can do the next time to increase your chances of being considered for the job. Even if you get a rejection letter, respond to it promptly in a positive manner. A timely, gracious, and professional response enhances your networking ability and might even help you be considered for another job in the same company or with a subsidiary of the firm in the future. I have seen many candidates who didn't get a position, but they conducted themselves with a professional demeanor and showed a positive attitude and were later contacted by the client or referred to a related company for another great job opportunity.

5. Grow Your Professional Skills with Courage and Creativity

Don't believe that you should simply apply for the next job or a better job with the exact skill sets that you currently have. Stretch yourself to apply for that dream job, even if your passion is in a related field. Make a courageous move to take online classes or attend additional trainings to demonstrate to your next employer that you are constantly evolving and growing your professional skills. Reach out to a family friend or previous boss or coworker to brainstorm about what skills and abilities would enhance your capabilities and interests. When an employer sees a candidate's resume who is constantly learning, innovating, and pushing themselves to become more professionally skilled, they will see that you are ready for a new opportunity in an expanded area of your career path.

6. Help Someone Else Who Wants to Learn What You Know

When we take the time to help another grow and develop, our own self-worth grows. There is a benevolent reward we all can achieve when we take the time to help someone else in need without any expectation of a personal or professional benefit. I do much mentoring at the college level, and I remember when my mentee called to tell me he got an amazing internship. I was so happy for him, but the sense of pride and fulfillment I got from taking the time to share my knowledge with that individual was incomparable. You expand who you are as a human being when you can selflessly help someone else who might be struggling or severely challenged.

When employers ask candidates what they are most proud of in the achievement area and those candidates talk about assisting someone else in a personal or professional endeavor, the employer often translates this to mean that the applicant will be a strong team player who will make a valuable contribution to the organization.

Start by listing all the ways you help or assist or support or bring value to others and then reflect on that list. Are those activities work-related or personal? Shift your mindset to be determined to make the most out of every opportunity, good and bad, and don't only strive for the ones that are comfortable and easy. Do everything you do with quality, excellence, and pride and see how it affects your self-worth and your ability to make a good living.

Feeling good about who you are and overcoming challenges sets a more positive tone on your internal compass, and your confidence and self-esteem radiates for all to see. As author Joshua Becker writes, "The wages that we earn provide for our lives, but they do not define our lives." Only YOU define your life. When you decide to be the best version of yourself you can be and commit to strengthening your own sense of worthiness and self-esteem, you will be amazed at what personal and professional success comes your way!

Become your best self by making a determined investment in yourself to be able to make a valuable contribution to the world at large.

Mary Ann Faremouth

Mary Ann showcases her talent and knowledge of the recruiting world in her current book, *Revolutionary Recruiting*, and the accompanying workbook, *Revolutionary Reinvention*. These books support individuals and corporations, teaching them how to tap into each candidate's unrealized potential to find the right person for each job, maximizing both employee satisfaction as well as the employer's bottom line. In 2020, she refocused her skills as a consultant, available to assist both the applicant and the client to quickly adapt to the new work world. She utilizes her platform as a writer and speaker and through her articles and affiliations to reach those in need of help, offering hands-on guidance to navigate this uncharted territory.

Mary Ann offers virtual and in-person workshops to personally guide individuals through personalized self-discovery to find better-suited career paths for success. Currently, she is reaching individuals through virtual avenues for universities and one-on-one mentoring for students soon to be out in the new work world. She continues to build her affiliations with recognized leadership organizations in order to best serve her clients and applicants by building a network of highly professional contacts throughout the world.

Facebook: **https://www.facebook.com/maryann.faremouthsandland**
Website: **https://faremouth.com/**
Books:
Revolutionary Recruiting **(https://faremouth.com/revolutionary-recruiting)**
Revolutionary Reinvention **(https://faremouth.com/revolutionary-reinvention)**

Wealthy Gina,
May you always have access to Abundance on Demand
Rita x.

FEELING SECURE WITH MONEY
BY RITA ROUSHDY

I've been broke doing work I loved...

And absolutely miserable earning a ton of money doing work I didn't even like.

As a money mindset and manifestation expert, I'm wholeheartedly devoted to helping established coaches release their deepest, subconscious blocks around finances, so they can earn reliable five-figure months and actually enjoy the abundant income they're creating.

I jumped into entrepreneurship at age twenty-two for the same reasons as you: time and financial freedom and location independence.

I started by following my dream to become a fashion designer. I adored the work, but I was barely making ends meet. So, I chased the money and got into clothing manufacturing instead. I ended up making the money–a lot of it–but it came with a price; I had built a business that tied me down to a daily routine filled with tasks I didn't like!

The golden handcuffs. I was trapped.

Queue a pandemic that took away all my in-person business overnight, and I was literally forced to make a change.

I realised that my external issues with money came from a much deeper (and a lot more mysterious) place... the subconscious mind. I was unhappy and unconfident in my abilities. I was using my work as a way to 'prove' myself because the harder you work, the more money you make, right? (This turned out to be wrong, actually!) I now realize that this behavior came from years of conditioning that I had inherited from my parents, which was no longer serving my highest good.

I dove all in to figure this out—dissolving my subconscious blocks and trauma around money, raising my vibration to one of unwavering self-belief, and learning how to support others with these techniques that had made such an incredible impact on my life.

"Easy Come, Easy Go."

My dad had a printing business in Egypt, where my mum and I often went to pitch in. I saw him get angry and frustrated when clients came in to check out the service, get samples, and then go ahead and decide to go with a competitor anyway. This is a memory I had to work on deeply, to break that pattern in my own life and business.

Let me start from the beginning... I grew up witnessing my dad (and uncle), as our sole breadwinner at the time, have businesses. I believe this had an influence on how I was naturally programmed, which led to me falling in love with having my own business at twenty-two right out of university.

This is how I naturally excelled at business from such a young age, where many women will have their money paradigm set to "I earn money through a nine-to-five job" and struggle making business work. This is because they simply don't hold the blueprint that supports the life they now have or desire to have.

The way in which my dad worked his fingers to the bone was mirrored into my own behaviour in how I ran things for the first eight to nine years of my adult life in business. This cemented into my paradigm that "You have to work hard to receive money."

Throughout my childhood, I saw how hard my dad worked for money. How he had to hustle to provide for us. And yet how much we continued to live in lack. Somehow, no matter how hard he worked, it felt like he still continued to feel like there wasn't enough to go around to provide for us, his family. To be able to reinvest back into the business for growth or even to feel like there was an abundance of money in the business to pay his staff.

I remember my mum having the mantra, "easy come, easy go," which began to ring into my ear a year or so after beginning to work on myself. The receptive manner of the mantra became ingrained into my being, buried into my subconscious and energy fields, and on a cellular level. It was literally a part of my biology until I decided to choose differently. This took a lot of deep subconscious work as well as other surface-level modalities that supported me in fully dissolving it from my field.

I remember seeing my dad's self-sacrifice and having the deep need to control, which was also a part of who I became when I started my first businesses. I used to sacrifice my sleep, my time, my energy in service of money. I put money on a pedestal.

In hindsight, every single thing I captured from my perception as a child became my reality in so many more ways than one.

This was my story until I decided to uncover and fully work on the deep subconscious programming that created my reality. This continues to be a process I do to this day that supports me in shaping the reality I desire.

A reality that I choose to create instead of one that's manifested from automatic past conditioning... A seven-figure coaching business that has a profound impact on the lives of millions of people across the world...

'Bye Overspender
Welcome Mindful Spender

Most people might go to societal programming to numb emotions with "retail therapy." But for me, it showed up slightly differently, no doubt due to what I saw modeled to me growing up.

I remember the time I used to eat my feelings. I would feel sad or lonely and my impulse was to turn to takeaway food, which was terrible, not only for my bank balance, but also for my emotional and mental state. It prolonged my healing because I was pushing my feelings further down and avoiding them.

Through my experience, I've realised how detrimental this is to my overall relationship with money. I found that the feeling of satisfaction that came from the moments I enjoyed the burger or pizza passed rather quickly. And once that hit of dopamine was gone, I quickly realised that the sadness, loneliness, or anxiety came right back.

That in that moment, food wasn't actually what I needed or wanted. And that after, I was left feeling even worse because I had wasted my money (and calorie intake) for a momentary feeling of relief. And when I'd come around and want to spend money on something I truly wanted and needed for myself or business, the money wasn't there to support me, which affected my sense of trust within my relationship with money. I needed to explore this cycle more deeply.

Here are some of my lessons from this time of my life, and what I now do as ritual to support me in becoming a mindful spender.

Emotional spending is one of the reasons why you're not enjoying the money you make.

You'll find yourself feeling satisfied for one minute, then realise it wasn't actually what you needed or wanted at that moment in time. Instead, take a moment to check in before you spend.

HALT
Are you Hungry?
Are you Angry?
Are you Lonely?
Are you Tired?

Use these questions before going full steam into "retail therapy" mode. Check in with yourself and figure out whether there's an emotional trigger around feelings that are coming up. Maybe you've programmed yourself or have been programmed as a child, or by society, to numb these feelings with shopping. If so, the shopping will only numb you momentarily until the trigger/emotions are dealt with.

To momentarily feel better, only to realise, oh, I still feel sad, or I still feel lonely, once the hit of dopamine is gone, which is also one of the reasons you may FEEL like there's not enough money to go around or do the things you truly want... because of unconscious spending, without realizing, in a moment of triggered state, when you're not thinking clearly.

Now, if it's not an emotional trigger that's behind the urge to buy or invest in something,

if it's something you truly desire, that will add something to your life. And the thing it adds could be a feeling of expansiveness, and abundance. (Although I'm a huge subscriber to the belief system of feeling abundant from within and not relying on external things to achieve that state of abundant being.)

Is it an investment in yourself that will better your life, your emotional, or mental state?

Is it an investment in your business that will support your growth?

Once you work on your emotional triggers and not go straight into retail therapy mode, you'll be in a position of having more than enough in the bank to enjoy the things that add true value to your life instead of a hit of momentary dopamine.

You'll be in a position to truly enjoy the money that you make. You'll be in a position to have your money go so much further because it's being used in a much more mindful way.

Through the healing work I did with money, I found myself working on my relationship with myself. It supported my growth in becoming unwaveringly confident. Radically increasing my self-esteem and the income that I'm now creating effortlessly is actually a bonus. Because I found true freedom from within. I found myself. Who I was always meant to be. A woman who is not dependent on external people or things to make her feel whole, momentarily, until said person or thing disappears.

As humans, through our primal need for survival, we naturally and unconsciously pass down our life lessons, our fears, and insecurities. The way we deal with money is a big part of that. We teach our kids what not to do, how to behave in certain situations, which are all filtered through (mostly) fear perceptions that we made up about life, ourselves, or money.

This affects our children's behaviour only to repeat and manifest another version of our lives, fears, and insecurities into theirs. And therefore, forces a repeat. But what if it didn't... what if we passed down expansive beliefs of effortless abundance, radical self-worth, unwavering self-confidence...

We hold the power to no longer carry these generational beliefs forward. So our kids, grandkids, and great-grandkids have no need to suffer the way our parents did. We have a magnitude of an opportunity to heal. To upgrade our belief system so that it no longer gets passed down unconsciously.

The opportunity of a lifetime lies in your hands. Will you choose to evolve or to repeat?

Rita Roushdy

Rita Roushdy is the founder of Abundance On Demand® Specializing in Money Mindset, and Manifestation Energetics. She helps established coaches and service providers feel confident and connected to their infinite state of abundance. She supports them in releasing the constant worry and anxiety around money and helps them feel financially secure in their businesses so they can generate consistent five-figure months.

My clients are able to buy their new cars in cash and feel abundant in doing so. They travel the world and experience new cultures whilst running their multi-six-figure businesses.

They can feel good taking time off and going on holiday whilst their businesses continue to generate passive income.

www.abundanceondemand.co.uk
rita@abundanceondemand.co.uk
https://www.instagram.com/abundance_on_demand/
https://www.linkedin.com/in/ritaroushdy/

FINDING MEANING IN IT ALL

LOVE-HATE RELATIONSHIP WITH MONEY
BY JACQUELINE CLARKE

This book is going to forever change me. I have a love-hate relationship with money. I love it when I have it and I hate it when I don't. A relationship with money is very powerful and emotionally charged. Money is important—it affects our self-esteem, security, and self-confidence. I don't know if many of you can relate to this or not.

I grew up in an era when men were the controlling factor in handling money. They were the breadwinners who were supposed to support their families. My dad's favorite phrase was, "take care of your pennies and your dollars will take care of themselves." As a young child, I could not really relate. Money was not discussed as many other things in our family were not discussed. My father took care of paying the bills and saving, making sure he took care of all our necessities. So, I never knew much about money growing up as a child.

My father worked two jobs for fifteen years of my childhood to provide for our family. My mother worked as well. I knew from my mother how important money was by her achievements in getting perfect attendance at work. So, there was a trait that was instilled in me. I remember as a child how important it was to work hard, be on time, and most importantly, be dedicated. Money was hard to attain. So having to work hard became very important to me and to making money.

With my first husband, I married into debt. I didn't realize what that was at the time. It was never discussed in my family. I didn't know how to deal with financial struggles while raising a family. In the beginning, my first husband

WOMEN, MONEY, AND INFLUENCE

was a great provider, then due to his health issues, he was unable to maintain employment. This resulted in us divorcing. I also at the time had two daughters. I worked two jobs during our marriage and while being a single parent. I worked in the medical field for approximately twenty-five years. I enjoyed working in the medical field, and I was able to learn a lot more about money and finances. I did medical billing, and surgery scheduling, and as office manager, I oversaw paying all the business bills, balancing the books, and posting payments.

In my second marriage, my husband was older than me. He was an excellent provider, which allowed me to spend more time with my family and grandkids. Also, he put me in charge of the finances. I did the best I could with the knowledge I had. My second husband passed away. Approximately forty days later, my oldest daughter, Jessica, passed away unexpectedly. I was now alone and raising grandkids.

I was now in another financial situation with the loss of my husband and daughter. Because of my own health reason and my husband's financial providing, I had not worked outside of my house in over ten years. I was introduced to network marketing. This was a whole new world to me, having different streams of income. Most importantly, I could work my own schedule. That allowed me to take care of my own personal health, and to take care of my grandkids. I was able to transport them back and forth to school each day.

I do what I do through network marketing. I do it to add another stream of income, for personal fulfillment, and to help my family. It is amazing to have the opportunity to network, connect, and grow my income. Network marketing not only helped me financially, but it also gave me back a life. People believed in me when I didn't believe in myself. I most definitely took much better care of my health as well. I came out of my comfort zone many times. At times, it was very difficult to deal with all the financial obstacles that arose, especially when I was raising my grandkids financially by myself.

I realized I was in the same footsteps as my father. I took care of everything to not burden my grandkids, and most importantly, I wanted them to not have to worry. I went to school and graduated high school. This not only boosted my self-confidence, but I was also trying to set examples for my grandkids. I wanted them to always work hard for what they wanted and needed, but most importantly, what they deserved. Do not give up when times are difficult. I choose to preserve when I was dealing with my own personal, tough financial situations. I believe, in doing so, it›s made me a stronger woman today.

I believe we women have no problem paying for services. Whether it may be a nail appointment, a massage, a haircut or going to breakfast, lunch, or dinner with our girlfriends. We pay for what we want, desire, and deserve. At times, we fall short by not charging for our own services. I believe at an early age we were taught that we take care of others before ourselves. I personally have always had a mindset of a caretaker from early on in my life. I attribute this to being of service to others. This was what I was taught as a child, mostly by my parents and a few family members. Today, more women are owning businesses. We, as other women, should encourage them, we should support, encourage, inspire, share our financial difficulties, and how we overcame them. When we can learn from another, it can be so empowering. Most importantly, be there for each other to celebrate their wins as well as their losses. We can help ourselves and others by eliminating self-sabotage with just a few suggestions: set calendar reminders, set up automatic payments, spend less than you make, always pay yourself first, make savings a priority, and make and follow a financial plan.

I have a few money success stories of my own. For me personally, looking back to when I was in my younger years, I always had financial worries. The older I got, the jobs I worked at, having met business-like-minded people helped in me better understanding finances. When I met and married my second husband, he took care of me and my family financially. For the first time, I didn't have to work, and I certainly had little or no worries. I had total financial freedom for the first time in my life. My parents often would say they no longer had to worry about me. They saw me struggle being a single parent. It was refreshing to hear this from my parents. My granddaughter, Daysia, expressed to me, after seeing me go through some financial setbacks, "if Papa was here, everything would be just fine." This comment was one that led me to start receiving money more easily from others. I was willing to do so to provide for my family. We are a team, taking care of one another. I realized by this time in my life that money could never buy happiness, but it does buy security and safety. If you can't pay cash for it, don't buy it; we do need money to pay for all the things that make life possible. The best thing to do with your money is to pay off debts. Stay out of debt and save.

I do believe that in different cultures, men and women have arrived at their own different beliefs in money. My childhood reflects a lot of my beliefs in finances and money, as it did in my earlier years. Finances and money were never discussed amongst children. My culture was that you didn't discuss adult situations with children. My parents' way of communicating so that we did not know what they were discussing or talking about things was to speak in Spanish. It was their way of communicating so that we did not know what they were discussing. I just knew that they worked hard and paid the bills. And by no means were we rich; we were middle class. I know that my parents had financial struggles while raising three small children very close in age.

I look forward to fully retiring next year on my birthday, June 13, and going out with a bang. I will be purchasing a mansion with two swimming pools, one indoor and one outdoors. It's large enough for my family and friends to come and visit.

Money doesn't buy happiness; it buys security and safety. We need to pay for all the things that make the life you want possible. I believe the best uses of your money are to:

- Use your money and pay all your debts.
- Stay out of debt!
- Invest wisely and make your money grow!

In closing, I would like to dedicate this chapter to Women of the World, Pleasant Hill Chamber, Laura Cartwright, massage therapist, and Daniel & Kathy Sitzmann (Sitzmann Chiropractor Care).

Jacqueline Clarke

Jacqueline Rose Clarke loves life. Some of the proudest moments in her life were becoming a mother, grandmother, and great-grandmother. She has raised kids for over forty years.

She joined the Walnut Creek chapter of Women of the World Networking in 2019. She is a former Pleasant Hill Ambassador, BNI–Stockton Member, and Concord Soroptimist.

She recently relocated to Arizona to pursue her career in health and wellness, to continue her own personal healing and transformation, and to share with others her own personal trials and tribulations.

She hopes to inspire others. She is an entrepreneur with Vasayo, as well as a brand partner. Jacqueline is a health enthusiast who enjoys working out, walking, running, and swimming. Her pastime is being with her family. Her motto is, "You Can Change YOU!" She's an overcomer.

Facebook: **https://www.facebook.com/Jacqueline.clarke9619**
Instagram: **vasayo_products_jclarke_**
Business page: **http://jclarke.vasayo.com**
Email: **jbaby1960@yahoo.com**

WOMEN AND MONEY: QUICK REMINDERS
BY NATALY KOLCHEV

Financial Health Helps Our Physical and Spiritual Health

When speaking about health, health can be divided into physical, spiritual, and financial health. Being financially healthy will in turn help your physical and spiritual health. Having several businesses and investments in my life, I discovered that our financial health benefits our spiritual and physical health. I'd like to talk about some of the money secrets that helped me in my life.

Little Secrets that Bring Big Results

Some of the wisdom secrets from my own family are acquiring quality things like clothes, household items, and cars because they can serve you longer than things that are cheap or just cost less money. I learnt this from my mother who taught me to invest in quality even if it is more expensive. It is better to have fewer things, but high quality versus a lot of low-quality items. I found that quality items can serve you way longer than cheaper things you can buy because they cost less.

Investing in Items that Can Bring Returns

Any car, equipment, or device is an equipment for making money, ex: sewing machine: can sew something and make clothes and sell. Another example is having a car; you can make money as a taxi and charge for it. Saved money is the earned money.

Importance of Planning and Saving

Have you heard this saying, "Those who can save can never be hungry"? In any type of business, as well as in the wealthiest households, saving and planning are very important.

There are a lot of ways to plan your money for the future. If you have kids, it is important to allocate for kid's college, and there are a lot of ways we can do that today. Consider planning for your own future as well. Daily and monthly planning is very important as well, especially for bigger expenses like housing, cars, etc.

Once you have your plan in place, it is important to have all the details of your planning listed in place and to break it down into details so that you can easily act on them. For example, if you plan to buy a car, the first action will be allocating the amount you can use for the down payment; second, planning the gas expenses for your car; third, researching insurance companies, etc.

When we are planning ahead, there is a good formula you can use that I learnt from Robert Kiyosaki. First, take your desired age you want to live by. For example, you plan to live to be one hundred years old. Second, deduct your current age; let's imagine you are twenty-five years old today. Example: 100-25=75, so 75 percent is your resources percentage. This is what you have so that you can use this percentage aggressively because you have a lot of time to invest aggressively and reap benefits. For those who are older than seventy years old, using 30 percent accordingly, according to this example, is key. If you are fifty years old, you will have 50 percent, you can use half of your income, but then reinvest the other half of this income somewhere, such as real estate purchasing; your income growth should exceed inflation as a minimum.

Pool Formula

Classic formula of the pool that has pipes that bring water to the pool and pipes that clean water out of the pool. Every purse and wallet we have is our own private pool, and maybe these deposits can be in crypto, company stocks, etc., or actual cash. There are pipes that help bring clean water and income deposits, in our case to your wallet and your pocket, but then there is water that is going out too, meaning money going out and taking out cash. Of course, we need to have that too as we need to eat, need to buy food, clothing, and other basic needs.

Sometimes, if we have extra cash, we can share the money with others, through donations, church donations, hospital donations, or paying someone for little jobs like walking dogs, cutting grass, but this way you are also sharing your income with others. This way, you can save your time and help others make money.

I also value this topic and the ability to pay for services because our time is more important than money. If you can pay others to complete some of the services in your household so that you can spend your time on other valuable things in your life, your time is spent with high quality.

Be Aware of Different Advice Out There

There are a lot of advisers out there, listen to other people's advice, but always check on your own, do your own research, and follow reliable advice and common sense. You've probably heard a phrase, "Say good-bye to your money easily," but I think for people to do so, we need to have enough first for ourselves before we can easily say good-bye to our money. Listen to advice, do your own research, collect information, and make your own decisions based on your circumstances. It is our own individual, personal responsibility to take care of our own money, so that we are able to provide for ourselves in establishing the life we want and then help others in need as well.

Nataly Kolchev

Born in Vladivostok, Russia, Nataly Kolchev lives with a motto, "You must know, everything will turn out well, even if everything does not turn out as planned."

She is a poet, a screenwriter, and an artist. Today, she lives in Sacramento, California. She gets inspired by reading inspiring books and through her travels. She was recently featured in the Russian documentary called *Sincerely Yours*, where she spoke about her life and success. She wrote one of her poems while flying to San Francisco from Russia. Her favorite quote is, "Inside each one of us is a little child that needs attention."

https://www.facebook.com/nata.kolchev.7
https://www.instagram.com/kolchevnata/

NEW SHOES
BY BONNIE M. RUSSELL

I always had a hard time with money. There. I said it.

I grew up with nothing, or rather, I grew up with nothing extra. We always had a roof over our heads, but my father didn't earn much and what extra he had, he spent on one of his expensive hobbies.

I grew up in the '70s, which means my parents were raised by survivors of the Great Depression, so a scarcity mindset got passed down to them... which got passed down to me. Clothes shopping was so rare that I only have one memory of buying them , and that was as a teenager. When I got too tall for my jeans, my mother would sew strips of material around the bottoms of the pant legs. Don't feel too bad for me, though. It was the ' 70s, and we all had patched up dungarees, so I didn't stand out too much.

My brother, sister, and I would only get new shoes for the first day of school, so we bought them a size too big. The only exception to this was when my brother put holes in his sneakers; he would get a new pair. I saw that happen and thought, *Hey! I want new sneakers, too!* and I remember getting on my bicycle, going really, really fast, then dragging my toes on the pavement to put holes in them so I could get a new pair.

I think that only worked out for me once.

Toys were also few and far between, so we took very good care of the ones we had. We learned the value of a dollar and we *made do*.

The funny thing is, that as bad as all that sounds, I have great memories of my childhood. We always had a meal on the table (powdered milk counts, right?), and my father almost always had a job. We never really *needed* anything.

Growing up with hand-me-downs and paper routes was the norm in my neighborhood. I was always happy, and I always had enough. Not plenty, but enough.

I got married at nineteen to a working man who kept a roof over our heads and food on the table, but not much more. We didn't go on vacations except for the occasional weekend at the Jersey shore with our two boys. Wonderful memories of time spent on the beach and walking the boardwalk, but stinging humility when the boys asked to play a game or asked for an ice cream cone, and we had to tell them, "Sorry, we don't have the money for that. We have games and ice cream at home."

It's the little things.

As bad as I felt, I never thought it would ever be any different. *That's just enough how things are* I told myself. *I'm not special enough to have more than 'just enough.' I have the necessities and I'm grateful.*

As a young married mother, it was a point of pride for me to take a few pantry staples and make them stretch as far as possible. It's not a cliché that whatever you give a woman, she will multiply it and give it back to you. Coming up with a nutritious meal for four was a magnificent triumph every time I did it!

It didn't occur to me that I could do something about it until I began to shift all my thoughts about my spiritual abundance to my finances. You see, I have amazing relationships, perfect health, and I love what I do, so I really thought that was all I had the right to ask for in this lifetime. I had a belief about money scarcity that I never questioned, and to add to that, I work in a profession where those who charge for their 'gifts' are ostracized by some in the healing community.

When my clients come to me about their relationship issues, it always amazes me how they could get themselves into such unpleasant situations. Situations that I would never put up with or even entertain! When they come to me with health issues ranging from weight concerns to diabetes to cancer, I think, *I would never allow my health to deteriorate like that.*

Then one day something clicked.

I hired a business coach for my little healing practice, and she told me that I needed to charge for my expertise. She said that I am worthy of receiving money, the same way I am worthy of receiving love and good health.

I started to notice that there are people in this world who live fearlessly regarding finances. Their mindset is such that they will always have shopping sprees, vacations, new cars, and just about anything they want, any time they want it. It occurred to me that I needed to start thinking about money the way I think about everything else in my life. I've got to believe - with all that I am - that I will have financial abundance the same way I have abundance in every other aspect of my life. And if I don't, it's because I'm out of alignment with the clear thoughts and emotions that will produce that kind of life for me.

The same way that I won't entertain thoughts about arguing with my husband or contracting an illness is the way I need to think regarding my pocketbook.

After several months of thinking thoughts of abundance and seeing very little change, I saw a colleague for a hypnosis session to uncover my hidden blocks. Hypnosis is an amazing tool because absolutely everything that we have ever seen, heard, felt, or experienced gets stored in the subconscious mind. I use it in my own healing practice because it is through hypnosis that we can root out limiting beliefs.

In my session, she asked me to go to the 'point of pain', the origin point or event of my belief in scarcity. In a flash I was five years old, sitting at the kitchen table, and my father was telling me that I could not have a quarter for the cereal breakfast party in my kindergarten class. He said that we couldn't afford it and that I couldn't have it. What I felt in that moment was red-hot embarrassment. I felt it in my face and in my ears and I felt it in my solar plexus. I felt unworthy. I felt ashamed. Seeing and feeling those emotions so clearly helped me to understand why I have trouble attracting money.

Once that limiting belief was revealed, I was able to process it and let it go. I could see it clearly for the nonsense that it was and replace the old belief with a new, healthy understanding that I am worthy of anything that I desire, including money.

This is what I do, every day, to reinforce my belief in abundance. I write these words in my journal: "I am so happy and grateful because I have multiple streams of income, perfect health, 20/20 vision, and the love of my life." As I write these words, with a pen on paper (not on the computer), I focus my energy on creating a vision of my future self. The version of me who has all of these things, and I concentrate on feeling the emotions of satisfaction and fulfillment. What this practice does is create a powerful, nonresistant thought/emotion process that calls my ideal self to me, and the longer I can hold that vision and feel the accompanying emotions, the more powerfully I am creating my future. This clarity is the powerful force behind the Law of Attraction.

If I could offer you any advice, dear reader, it would be this: seek professional assistance to get to the root of any belief in scarcity and do it sooner rather than later. Don't waste another day worrying about how you're going to pay the bills, because, trust me, it doesn't take time, it just takes alignment. I knew this, but I wasn't asking myself the right questions to uncover this belief in scarcity. Once I hired someone else to ask the questions, the Benjamins began to flow like crazy! Then create a vision of your future self that is thriving and doing all the things you want to do. Go out into the world wearing the clothes you can see her wearing, eating the foods that she eats, and carry yourself the way she does. Talk to people with the confidence she has and this will call her to you. First, practice these things in your mind, then do them. Before you know it, you will BE her.

Practice doesn't make perfect; practice makes habit. Practice being the person you wish to be, and you can't *not* become her.

I am more her every day, and you know what? I am overflowing. I will always have plenty. Whenever I want to travel across the country to visit family, I can.

If I want a new dress, I can just go buy one.

Today, I have the greatest sneakers that money can buy. And if they get holes in them, I can buy more!

Bonnie M. Russell

Rev. Dr. Bonnie M. Russell, speaker, author, and healer-trainer

Bonnie is a doctor of shamanistic theology. She has been in private practice since 1998 and she's been training intuitive healers since 2011.

AllOne Sacred Services Healing Academy is a professional training center that enables coaches, healers, and holistic health practitioners to

WOMEN, MONEY, AND INFLUENCE

master their gifts so they can attract premium clients and make a difference in the world.

Bonnie helps people to remember that, at our core, we are happy, curious souls who sometimes experience sadness, but we are not sad. When we experience traumas or illness, these are just signals from the subconscious that we have forgotten our true nature, which is pure joy.

Go to **Linktr.ee/BonnieMRussell** to learn more about Bonnie.

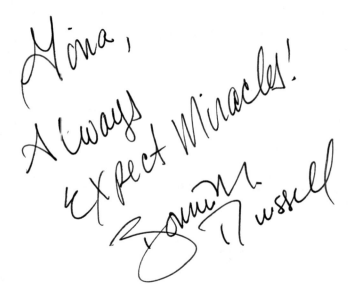

FROM DARKNESS TO SUNLIGHT
BY AKILI ATKINSON

There is a quote by S.E. Hinton that framed a large portion of my life. "When I stepped out into the bright sunlight, from the darkness...." Although I was not coming out of a movie house, I was leaving a twenty-year marriage. The sunlight brought the realization of the magnitude of what was happening. I had $50.00 in my bank account, one child in college, and another a senior in high school. Up to this point, my children had enjoyed a life of comfort. Both were highly competitive athletes, which required a lot of time and money. I never worried about how these expenses would be paid because I had a supportive husband who agreed with empowering them to thrive in whatever arena they chose. They were free of financial worry when they decided to try a new endeavor. This was all about to change. Now I sat allowing the sunlight to dry my tears as I thought, *how did I get to this point?*

Why Didn't I Listen to my Parents?

It is hard to talk about money and how your parents introduced you to the concept without sounding as if they should take some blame for your struggle. My upbringing started from a fairly traditional standpoint. Even though I was adopted as a baby, there was no difference in the rearing of myself and my brothers. We all were able to wake up to the smell of waffles or pancakes for breakfast before school. My mother stayed at home while my father put his suit on every day and headed to the bus stop, leaving the family car for my mother if she needed it. We did not get a ride to school because, in those days, a mile to walk was not that unusual. Looking back, it was the start of what would be my toxic relationship with money. I don't remember asking too many questions about how money was spent when I was young. I learned the value of money meant you don't spend it until you need to and when you do, it will be after researching *Consumer Reports* to make sure you are getting the best value. The inquisitive child I was missed the 'why' and I was resigned to this being the, "because I said so" subject.

Watching my mother enjoying time with us after school and my father walking through the door just in time for dinner every night, it seemed to me, if you worked hard, comfort would follow. My brothers and I never went without what my parents thought we needed. This would become very important as I entered my teenage years.

Financing a Teenager

I always thought I needed a new outfit, more makeup, or the latest Stevie Wonder album. My brothers did not share my vision of wanting every item available at the mall, and they were resigned to the life that was provided.

As an obstinate teenager, many of the lessons about money were suddenly lost on me. I wanted to spend frivolously on the latest clothing trend. My father and mother would share their fear of dangerous overspending but never with details that worried me. The relationship with money began to unravel with no end in sight.

I entered college already in debt and felt like there was no way out. Dropping out seemed easier than finding a solution. I would calculate the payments needed to pay off the credit card debt quickly. By this time, it was too late, and because I gave up, I started a cycle of minimum payments that would last over fifteen years. The information instilled in me when I was young wasn't lost on me, but I had gone so far away from the teachings, I felt hopeless. I did not think I was the only one who spent more money when they started feeling anxious, sad, nervous, or even happy. It was a quick way to escape the realities of the world.

Entering the Real World

This was a cycle that had no end. As if the feeling of despair could not get any worse, the expense of children compounded the struggle. With my husband, at the time, on board, we began the long road to paying off all our debt. I could see the reason because, looking into the eyes of our children, I knew they needed a strong example of financial stability. The importance of having savings and being secure had a reason, my kids. We needed to begin to guide our children in the ways of finance and that could not be done while drowning in debt.

With second jobs in place, we did well to pay down all the debt and started living a life of comfort. I have learned over the years that dealing with your finances is much like dealing with your health. Just because you get in shape doesn't mean you get to stop exercising and eating right. Even if you don't have debt, you must work on your financial plan because falling back into the trap is easy.

Justification Spending

Justification came easily as the children grew; private school and extracurricular items seemed a necessity. I don't remember how the credit card balances got high again, but I remember thinking it had happened overnight. The justification was easier than doing the work to figure out a solution that did not involve additional credit card debt. As the numbers crept up, disappointment set in again, and a sense of hopelessness was there. It was harder this time, the children were asking for their first car, college was around the corner, and I was never sure what my son was eating to continue to grow so much. Soon my husband would be retiring, and it looked like I would be working well into my seventies. During this time, I was able to see what it could look like if I followed the ideas my parents had about spending. No impulsive purchases and use cash as much as possible echoed in my head. I watched my brothers continue their comfortable lives, and my parents retired earlier than is usually possible. I wanted that for my family and was determined to change the direction of spending.

It was time to get on track again when the next blow not only knocked me off my feet, but it made it almost impossible to manage my finances in my mind.

When Reality Set In

After twenty years of marriage, I found myself single, with only a high school diploma and a pile of justification that now didn't make any sense. I worked for a non-profit, helping individuals with disabilities find employment. As a supervisor, I didn't make much more than the people I was helping. With the latest tears in my eyes, I realized what needed to happen. If I was going to be broke, I was going all the way to beans-and-rice broke. With only myself to rely on, I didn't have the extra income that once provided the security to feed my spending. You are probably thinking at this point that my home was full of fine furniture and designer clothing. That is not how I spent money; my goal was to be comfortable and not go without anything I wanted. I attribute this to my childhood envy of others who had more than I did. My father was one of ten children and understood early on that without a positive relationship with money, trouble could happen at any time. He was determined to instill that in me even as I threw my latest tantrum.

After enrolling in college, I knew the lean years would have a positive outcome. It wasn't that I didn't know how to save; I never had the fear that I needed to take it seriously. Being in college at the same time as your children has its advantages, besides the added tax breaks. The college crew would visit on the weekend to talk about how they wanted their future to look. With my children leading the conversation, words like diversify, investment property, and savings were discussed regularly. They looked forward to the opportunity to put to use the lessons we taught them about money. As a proud mom sitting there, I knew my relationship with money would change for good. All of the teachings from my youth were there, and now I would implement new strategies to continue to be a positive example for my children. Any free time was spent scouring the Internet in search of even the smallest scholarship because every little bit helped. Five years later with my MBA in tow, I set out to change the world in corporate America. The goal was to make a lot of money and retire in time to hang out with my brothers and parents on Easy Street. It didn't take long for me to realize my life would be dedicated to service, and I probably wouldn't see the dollar amount I anticipated. My calling to help individuals with disabilities superseded any thought of money, which meant I had some decisions to make.

The Fear of Spending

Would I go back to credit cards and excessive spending because I didn't make the money I wanted or learn to live within my means? When I decided that helping others was more important, it was much easier to give up a lifestyle that was never mine to begin with.

What I found during this time of practicing patience, and being a good steward of money, I never went without anything I needed. When I structured my paychecks based on the priority to tithe, pay myself, and then my bills, I was more cautious with the money left over. Spending an exorbitant amount on something didn't feel as good anymore. I wanted tangible things that celebrated the hard work I was doing every day.

I tell my story about my struggles with money to bring awareness to why we are spending. Spending for me took me away from my responsibilities. I would justify the new blouse but never a new savings bond. Year after year, as I changed my lifestyle, took classes on spending, and taught others about spending, I continued to receive raises. One day I woke up and said, 'I want more than just holding my breath and hoping I get a raise.' I looked at my resumé and compared my accomplishments to job descriptions, and I began to say, 'I am worth more.' I wanted a balance where I was getting what I was worth so some of my money could go to the rewards. I needed to fight for what I deserved because now I would spend it the right way. I would make my checklist so I had a framework for any financial conversation because I would not be deterred from my goals and what I deserved.

When the Sunlight Began to Shine

I sat one day with an older friend and listened as she talked of her troubles. Her hands were worn from years of service work, yet she was still holding the designer bag on her shoulder. The need to work beyond her retirement age while flashing all her jewelry reminded me of the direction I was once headed. I looked into her eyes to see the fear of years of no financial responsibility. No longer do the fancy trinkets weigh the same when one is unable to produce a financial portfolio.

How could she have been helped earlier in life and what could I say to her now? Feeling sorry for someone does not produce a viable answer. Learning why the relationship with money is not productive is most important. In my work, I have an in-depth finance section for individuals with disabilities. I don't tell them to spend or not to spend. We talk about what are the long-term consequences of spending. How will your relationship with money grow as you mature? What will you need for your every five-year plan? Every five years can be the opportunity to celebrate major financial accomplishments or revise things that did not work. The stability of enjoying and saving must be realized to have true balance. I am thankful that I can buy nicer things now without much concern but I am more appreciative that I get an opportunity to give nicer things because that is more valuable than anything I have.

Akili Atkinson

Akili Atkinson is a neurodiversity trainer, certified purpose coach, and certified autism specialist. She is the owner of the consulting firm Akili's Corner, LLC.

Akili trains individuals and businesses to understand changing employment demands. Her expertise as a trainer and consultant spans over twenty years of professional integration, specializing in training, diversity inclusion, disability development, and technique implementation strategy. Her approach is impact-oriented, balancing compassion with discipline while delivering lasting results.

She is a Distinguished Toastmaster and an award-winning speaker, placing internationally in the Toastmasters International Speech Contest. As a doctoral candidate, she is focused on bringing adult education and workplace needs more closely aligned.

Akili brings fun and excitement into training, allowing for different learning styles to shine. Purpose and passion drive her work, and she is devoted to helping people realize their own life's purpose.

Linktr.ee/Akiliscorner

THANK YOU

Thank you for taking the time to read these amazing stories!

I wanted to share with you a little more about our Women of the World Network® community. Women of the World Network® is a supportive, entrepreneurial community for multinational and international ladies thriving all over the world. We support women of diverse cultures and backgrounds to build their unique lives and businesses. Our mission is to empower multinational and global entrepreneurial women to build unique businesses (and lives) in a new country based on their uniqueness, truth, and individuality.

Membership Highlights:

- Networking visibility, mindset, uniqueness for multinational women in business
- Twenty-one countries represented in the community
- One in every two members forms a partnership
- Receive one to two business referrals upon membership start
- Community where accents are in the mix. Let your accent help you get back to your roots and remind yourself who you truly are!

Our programs include community membership, strengthen membership, worthy and wealthy entrepreneur, multi-author bestselling series, networking events, and retreats.

Want to start your own Women of the World Network® chapter or join an existing one in our growing community?

WOMEN, MONEY, AND INFLUENCE

Check out our growing community here:

Our regions: **https://www.womenoftheworldnetwork.com/our-regions**
Our programs: **https://www.womenoftheworldnetwork.com/our-programs**
Facebook page: **https://www.facebook.com/WomenOfTheWorldNetwork**
Instagram: **https://www.instagram.com/womenoftheworldnetwork/**
Email us: **info@womenoftheworldnetwork.com**

TESTIMONIALS

"To be a 'Woman of the World' means to be a voice for women like me. I am representing women of my culture. It means being a part of a community of other empowered women. We all come together, from different backgrounds and cultures, and we celebrate and support each other."
—Maritza Levy

"To be a 'Woman of the World' means to be a woman who lives with confidence, commitment, and purpose to not only add value to her life but to share the value with others through service and standing in her power while doing it."
—Johnetta Cuff

"I have always strived to be a lifelong learner and what better way to educate myself in thriving in my own personal development, and as well as for my business by flying amongst other truly amazing women, who are like-minded, high achieving, and mostly genuine. From the E-Academy, the WOTWN Anthology, and a culture connected to celebrate our authentic diversity, there are numerous avenues to learn, connect, and most importantly, freely express your true identity as a woman. It's been over a year since I joined the Sacramento chapter along with Freya Krishnan as our chapter leader, and all the uniquely tailored topics you can learn from are endless. I am so glad I joined!"
—Marissa Cruz-Hernandez

WOMEN, MONEY, AND INFLUENCE

"I love having the support of this community, learning from, and empowering women. Can't say enough about the quality of women in this group! There is a genuine support system, coming to act at other's events, supporting each other's ventures."
　—Freya Krishnan

"What it means for me to be a 'Woman of the World'? I believe we are all unique women. I believe I am connected to a greater and bigger beautiful picture and that we are all connected to serve a greater purpose. I believe that our individual uniqueness and my uniqueness serves a greater good."
　—Kendra Jefferson

"Women of the World Network® is a community that is truly created around a recipe for success that includes elements of the community framework of personal fulfillment, professional growth, and individuality. In addition, I truly get a sense of community and sisterhood being a member of Women of the World Network®."
　—Mary Ann Faremouth

REVIEWS

"Sometimes books find you at just the right time, but what I love about this book is that instead of worrying about timing, these women are encouraging others to dare to dream. Even if that dream hasn't gone as you planned. The advice they give is heartwarming and focused on spirituality and being intentional to all parts of life. My favorite part, none of these stories are like mine, yet I can find similarities and hope in each message. It was just the motivation I needed to believe in myself first but also to remember that I don't have to go at it alone."
Tiffani Freckleton, RN and best-selling author of My NICU Story: Written With Love and Letters to a Future Nurse.
On Instagram @inspiredbynicu & @bookstagramandread

"For someone who grew up in a communist country, like me, with no role models of entrepreneurship around, reading this book has been a breath of fresh air.
These stories of real women from around the world, told by themselves in an intimate voice, gave me a sense of possibilities and a strong feeling that an abundant life is possible for everyone, regardless of their background.
Above all, it made it palpable for me that once we connect with a purpose beyond ourselves, we connect with abundance.
Last but not least, it gave me practical ideas that I look forward to following up with in my own life. «
Radha Alina Ionescu,
Conscious Love Coach,
Truth Makes It Intimate
www.TruthMakesItIntimate.com

WOMEN, MONEY, AND INFLUENCE

"This anthology is a timely collection of feminine wisdom around finance. From the collective experience of leaders around the world, readers receive empowering and applicable models for building wealth, not just in their portfolios, but also in their lives. An inspiring must-read for women of all ages!"
Shelby Kottemann, 2x Internationally Bestselling Author, Certified Reiki Master, Founder of Love's Nature LLC
shelbykottemann.com

"Elle Ballard's anthology Women, Money and the Energy of Life created a surge of energy in me while and after reading as the century of the woman is fully upon us and it's been a long time coming. The stories she collected are inspirational, revolutionary, invigorating, and spiritual. Elle's ability to preview these vignettes is superb. I am a proud, long-time Rotarian and pleased to announce that our Rotary International President, Jennifer Jones, is the first female president in our organization's 117-year history. The anthology is a highly recommended read for both men and women."
Terry Philip Wilson
Author: Miracle in the Mara, An Unforgettable Story of a Young Maasai Warrior's Vision
Tdub98@comcast.net

"From birth to death, our choices in our pursuit of happiness are as effective as our awareness of self and surroundings. These stories provide perspective on uncovering our blind spots and making the right choices. My favorite was the importance of awareness of our talents and financial independence in setting and achieving big goals."
Manisha Gupta | https://www.linkedin.com/in/manishagupta

"An international approach to living well and finding one's worth. The co-authors share their story of moving from struggle to wealth with a shift in mindset, recognition of self-worth and acceptance that women and money do align to achieve success and a life filled with abundance."
Maureen Ryan Blake
Maureen Ryan Blake Media Production

"This book is about an amazing group of women who went through many struggles, and through hard work, were able to create their dream life. I was inspired by the courage and motivation of these women to become masters of their lives. Their journey was not always smooth and easy, but they were able to learn and grow from their experiences. Their focus on creating a beautiful life came across in a powerful way which will help others know that a better life is possible."
Brita Peterson
Author
www.britapeterson.com

"Loved every story in the book and saw me in every chapter. What a treat it was to be one of the first ones to see how extraordinary women are around us and could see myself having a conversation with each one of them. I am envious that I am not among these women!"
Uttara Pandya
Director with Melaleuca
https://calendly.com/upandya/30min

"I recently had the pleasure of reading "Women, Money and Energy of Life" and it was truly inspiring! One of the most valuable takeaways from this book was the emphasis on choosing your own path in life. Overall, "Women, Money and Energy of Life" is a must-read for anyone who wants to take control of their financial future and create a life that's truly fulfilling. I highly recommend this book to anyone who wants to learn more about the relationship between money and happiness, and how to build a life that's aligned with your values and goals."
Fernanda Cortes
Graphic Designer |Canva Coach| Content Creator
info@thefernandasi.com

WOMEN, MONEY, AND INFLUENCE

"This book is very inspiring! I definitely can relate to it and I'm pretty sure that a lot of people will do too. Full of amazing stories and teaching and wonderful women. It makes me realize the true value of my own experiences, encourage me to start with a simple plan, learn from their ups and downs and hope for a brighter future. I hope that every woman (and man) will get to read this book!"
Margie Viaga Calangian
Litigation Support Specialist
Lieff Cabraser Heimann & Bernstein, LLP
www.lieffcabraser.com

Made in the USA
Middletown, DE
21 April 2023

29145798R00076